JOSEPHINE,

BEST TO YOU AS WE FIGHT FOR RACIAL
HEALING IN AMERICA. BLESSINGS!

COACH T (GREG THOMAS)
I COR. 9:24
JOSHUA 1:9

1-10-19

RACE IN AMERICA:
A CALL TO HEAL

outskirts
press

TABLE OF CONTENTS

FOREWORD

I met Coach T. at the Black Coaches Association gathering in Indianapolis a number of years ago. I found him to be highly energetic with a great work ethic and a passion for doing what is right. I am excited that he finally decided to write a book, because he has so much to share.

Greg has endured a lot through his life, and he always comes out of those experiences with a greater perspective, as well as a positive attitude. In my years of interacting with Coach T, I have discovered that his positive attitude has allowed him to learn from each of his experiences, whether they were good or bad.

He and I have dissimilar backgrounds, but we have the same passion. While I grew up in New York, the son of an NBA coach, he grew up in Kansas City, the son of a small business owner. My work for change is mainly in league offices, the NCAA, individual institutions of higher education and international sports organizations, while Greg's are in classrooms and athletic training fields for the youth of our country.

But we share many of the same opinions and goals, many of which are spelled out in the pages of this book. We believe that the color of one's skin has no bearing on their worth or ability to perform tasks.

I believe I know Greg's heart. His passion and purpose, like mine, is to end racial injustice. While I try to do that on a national and global scale, I know Coach T desires to do that one life at a time. That is really where it needs to start. You can't legislate equality. It needs to start with a grass-roots effort, led by passionate people like Greg Thomas.

This book will make a difference, not just in Greg's world in mid-America, but in much wider circles. It's impact will be felt for generations. He can be a resource for true change in our great nation.

Will you join him? It's a noble effort, and it starts with reading this book. You'll be glad you did.

Dr. Richard Lapchick
Director, The Institute for Diversity and Ethics in Sport

ACKNOWLEDGMENTS

This book is a compilation of experiences I have had in my 58 years on this Earth. Many of them have been good, a few great. But there have been plenty that have not been good. I hope I have learned from all of them, and I hope that this book can help us all learn.

I couldn't have gotten to this point in my understanding of race in America without the impact of many people. I want to take this time to give a few shout-outs.

I've been a coach and a teacher. I have come to appreciate so many fine teachers I've worked with at various schools. As a sub and then a para in the Shawnee Mission District, I was shown tremendous respect and given great support by the teachers at most of the schools. The teaching staff and students at Olathe Northwest High School worked great together to have a wonderful environment for learning. The teachers at Christ Prep Academy and Olathe Christian School did an excellent job of loving on staff and students to foster a great environment to teach kids to serve Christ all of their days.

On the sports side, my mentor and freestyle and Greco-Roman wrestling coach for several vital years was Chuck Sears of Blue Springs. I believe he is the best wrestling coach in the Midwest. I can't thank him enough for the wisdom and encouragement he has given me for close to 40 years. Chip Sherman, whom I believe is the best football coach in Missouri or Kansas, was the first coach under whom I coached football. His zeal and love for the kids and the game was infectious, and it has stayed with me for many years. His love of family, and his passion to have his players and staff to love and serve each other, was a great learning tool for me.

I've been extremely blessed to have worked with great coaches and families over the many years of coaching high school and youth sports. Karl and Andrea Wagner have meant the world to several of our programs. They've exemplified "agape" love for all of the families involved in our programs. Rob and Tina Behler have walked beside me for many years. We're so thankful for their love and support. Merc and Latonya Boyd have been a great inspiration for many years. The Dingmans, the Fords, the Beutlers, the Hummelgaards, the Diazs, and the Nelsons, and many more families gave it their all for others for period of time.

Our church families have been such a blessing to my family. Their input has helped us to overcome the trials and tribulations of life. Kansas City Fellowship/Metro Christian Fellowship, Eagle Creek Family Church, The River and Abundant Life have played strategic roles over the years. The wisdom and prayers of Mary King will never be forgotten.

Our home group, with families like the Siems, the Pughs, the Hills, the Dublins, the Guenthers and the Rackleys, was instrumental in helping us raise our three kids. Lots of prayer and encouragement were key to helping us make great decisions that shaped the childhoods of our kids so they all prospered spiritually, academically, athletically and socially. I believe if all young married couples had a home group in their lives, to be there for you in the tough and great times, we'd have more 30- to 50-year wedding anniversaries. There's something about doing life together that can give you a calm during the storm.

I appreciate my Durham School Services family, as we work together to serve the wonderful kids in the Blue Valley District. The training and support provided by Sean Burns and staff is exceptional.

Much love for my Uber riders from all over the globe who have given me great insight on how we can heal as a nation. It's been priceless to hear the hearts of people from big cities to very small towns. There's no way I could ever go to all the places that have been helpful, but my riders have taken me there with their words.

My mom and dad gave sacrificially so I could travel around the U.S to play sports, participate in FCA and to serve. I didn't appreciate my dad enough until later in life, but we had ample time to grow and appreciate each other. I knew every day of my life that my mom and dad loved me unconditionally—what we describe in this book as "agape love."

During their later years I'd take them to lunch or dinner to thank them for what they'd done for me and my siblings. I'd get to pray with them and make sure they realized that we'd get a chance to spend an eternity together since we've accepted Jesus Christ as our personal savior. This was so reassuring that when they died, it made it much easier to take care of all details in their cases.

My brother, Myron, has been an excellent coach on my staff. He has given me tremendous nuggets over the years and solid insight into this book. My sister, Marquitta (Thomas) Harrell, has always been encouraging to me as well. She also gave some great insight into this book.

My aunt, Dorothy (Dot) Williams, has been a great source of historical perspective. She has given me valuable info on the early years of my parents. She stepped up in a major way when my parents died five years apart. To this day, she gives me important nuggets that are inspiring to me.

The KC Gorilla Club has been a great support for my family, as two of our sons were Gorilla football players. Casey Casebolt, John and Dona

Collar, John Levra and the gang have been a constant source of support and fellowship.

Chad Jackson, a.k.a. "The Sports Guy," has been there during the ups and downs of coaching and life in general. Stephan "Stevo" Gordon has no idea of the great impact he's had on many, especially in Joplin during the Sports Camps. Ken Walton, a former Kansas student and baseball player gave a tremendous amount to the Lincoln Prep baseball squad that I was blessed to coach for four years.

There have been some wonderful people who've done major work in the area of racial reconciliation. I spent countless hours reading, listening and watching stories and testimonies to gain more wisdom in this area. Here is a short list of some that had a strong impact on me: Dr. Tony Evans, Matt Chandler, Voddie Baucham, Michael Emerson, Dr. Joy Degruy, Tim Wise, Jim Wallis, Michele Alexander, Dr. Robin DeAngelo, Dr. Michael Eric Dyson and Benjamin Watson. There are many others who have great insight into some of the complicated issues in dealing with Race in America.

After the Joplin tornado of a few years ago these families stepped up to show Stephan Gordon and me the kind of love that it speaks about in Leviticus 19:34: "The foreigner residing among you must be treated as your native-born. Love them as yourself, for you were foreigners in Egypt. I am the LORD your God."

These families were exceptional in showing the love of Christ for the kids in their recovery from the devastating tornado in 2011 during the Sports Camps. These are the families: Tom and Molly Hamilton, Ryan and April Bennett, Dave and Lisa Marbaugh, and Brad and Cindy Graves. Other people made our stays so rewarding. It was a powerful experience that many kids enjoyed. I'm so grateful to have met these wonderful people who spend their lives giving and serving others.

I met a guy more than a decade ago when I worked for the Kansas City FCA. He would write great stories for *Sharing the VICTORY* magazine. He knew many people around the U.S. After we each left the FCA staff, I rarely saw him. But I knew that when the time came for this powerful book to be written, he needed to be a huge part of it. David Smale is the guy and he's incredible in so many ways.

This book will be spectacular, due to his thought and insight in putting it together. He's been so instrumental from the tiniest to the largest details. The countless hours of editing and ideas have been very taxing on us both, but inspirational to me. Each chapter was a great effort. Many things were discarded, and in some cases a new approach was taken. If you ever need a writer or editor, he's a guy you'd want to consider. Of all the candidates I had to help with this project, I'm so glad and grateful that I chose David! And as a bonus, his son, David Lee Smale, did a great job with the cover photo/design. I remember young David when he was a camper at FCA camps. It's great to see him using his talents for God's purposes.

When you have three of the best kids on the planet, it's easy to give thanks to God for that and appreciate what they do for others. BreAnn Thomas Chang is our firstborn. She and her husband, Barry, have traveled the world serving many. As this book is being written, her family is living in Budapest, Hungary. She's served in places like Mexico and Jamaica, among others. She's been a huddle leader at FCA Camps, as have our boys, in order to give back for what they've received. She's also the mom of my three oldest grandchildren: Bailey Rae (9), Ellie Shu (4) and Kenzo Tae (2).

Our first-born son, Dr. Nathan Thomas, has also been far and wide to serve others. Nate helps people now as a chiropractor with his wife, Dr. Kara Thomas. He was an All-American at Pittsburg State University in track & field. He also played football there. He went to Rio Verde, Mexico, to serve kids there for FCA.

Our youngest, Jonathan Thomas, was always the youngest on Nate's teams growing up. He was the last to get to play, and many times he was shielded from the "tough stuff." But usually he found a way to get in the thick of the battle. He was part of a national championship football squad at Pittsburg St. in 2011. He earned a degree in Construction Management and now works with JE Dunn in Kansas City He and his wife, Sarah, have a treasure named Riley Jo (1).

Nate's graduation was a big day for the Thomas family.

All three of my kids have inspired me to do my best. They are great examples of what hard work and perseverance can do, especially when your work is dedicated to the Lord.

More than 36 years ago, Becky and I said, "I do." After three wonderful kids, and now four spectacular grandkids, it's time to reflect and give thanks to a loving God. Becky has been with me through all the things you'll read about in this book. She has been an anchor for me to keep on with a Galations. 6:9 type of mentality. She also has served FCA for many years and has helped people across the USA. I couldn't be more proud of and thankful for my Becky!

I've spent many years in research for this book, but resisted writing it until now. I thought that most couldn't or wouldn't relate to some of the things I've seen, since it wouldn't be in their experience or history. Could people actually empathize or comprehend some of the issues we bring up in this book? As we finished this book I'm realizing that many can and do. This makes it easier to share my heart.

I hope you enjoy this book. If I can come to your school or place of business to share, please contact me to work things out for a memorable visit and opportunity for us both to grow.

Blessings
Coach T
Email – coachttd@yahoo.com
Website – www.coachttd.com
Phone – 816-699-4985

Chapter 1

MY STORY

I WAS BORN in the late 1950s, which means I spent my "Wonder Years" in America in the 1960s. The tumultuous decade of the 60s to me meant spending my time playing whatever was in season. During baseball season, we played baseball. During football season, we played football. I never liked basketball, because I was always one of the shortest kids my age, but when everybody else was playing basketball, I played basketball too. Sports were important to me, as they represented the best way to establish myself among my peers.

I was aware there was a world going on around me. But, like most kids, the outside world didn't affect me too much. My parents taught my sister, Marquitta, (three years younger than I) and my brother, Myron, (another three years younger) that we should treat everybody with respect. It didn't matter what they looked like.

My concept of a problem with race was when I had to run against someone who was faster than I was. I wanted to beat the other kid. I was not real fast, but I was quick, so I won quite a few.

Besides the three of us, we usually had cousins living with or around us, so my parents had influence on a lot more than just the Thomas kids. They were very focused on making life as idyllic as possible for all of us. They hadn't grown up that way, and they wanted to make sure we had every opportunity to achieve our goals.

My parents, Charlie and Mattie Thomas, were born in the deep south, where Jim Crow laws were the norm. Dad was born December 21, 1936, in Lake Providence, Louisiana. Mom was born April 28, 1937, in Eudora, Arkansas. The two towns are less than 25 miles apart, so they were practically neighbors. When my Dad's family moved back to Eudora (where his Mom had grown up), he and my Mom started going to school together, probably midway through grade school.

Instead of school, athletics and other extra-curricular activities, their daily goals were based on who could pick the most cotton. Their families were sharecroppers, and it was "all hands on deck." They usually attended school only after the chores were done or the weather was too bad to be in the field. Sometimes school hardly was worth the effort, due to only being able to come to school very sporadically. Dad, especially, often was behind in the flow of school.

Mom remembered working from "Sun to Sun" or "Can to Can't," as the whole family worked very hard to make enough money to barely make ends meet. There was no time for leisure activities, like television or any kind of play.

The schools in Eudora were segregated, so they attended an all-Black school. Mom and Dad were ridiculed by their fellow students because they were from the country and couldn't keep up, and they wore run-down clothing. Their fellow students called them "cotton picking rabbits." Dad finally decided to stop fighting the battle, and he dropped out of school around the 10th grade.

Mom toughed it out and graduated from the Eudora (Colored) School in 1957, the same year of the "Little Rock 9," which happened just a few hours to the north. There's plenty to read in history books and on the Internet, but that was when a group of nine Black students decided that they should have the right to attend the same schools as their White neighbors in Little Rock, Arkansas. The unwritten laws of that day said differently, so when angry residents showed up to stop them and they called the local police, they got a deaf ear.

They turned to the state for help, but the reaction was the same. So this group of students appealed to President Dwight Eisenhower, who sent in the National Guard. The students were ushered into Little Rock Central High School by armed Guardsmen. This is what was shown on the news.

This didn't just happen on the first day of school. It happened all year long. Guards sat on opposite sides of the Black students to protect them from being beaten or harassed in class by their White classmates. Eventually the tension died down some, but it was a racially charged atmosphere before and after that year.

Many Black people from that area left that life as soon as they could, looking for the promise of a better life somewhere else. Some joined the Armed Forces, while many others headed to cities in the north to find work and perceived less discrimination.

The unknown was not as scary as the known, because the situation in which they lived was too much to bear.

With that knowledge and those goals, my parents moved to Kansas City as part of the "Great Black Migration," spoken of in the book *Warmth of Other Suns* by Isabel Wilkerson. It's hard to put a number on it, but my guess is that 95 percent of the decision to leave the south was because of racial hardship and the other 5 percent was economic. It's hard to differentiate between the two, because most of the economic hardship was because of race. But it was common for Black people to disappear because of the Klan or other similar groups. Going to the police for help didn't work, because many of the officers were part of the Klan or sympathized with their cause.

It was safer to escape the region and head north.

My Dad came to Kansas City first and quickly found a job in a factory. The work was hard, but not as hard as picking cotton, and the pay was significantly better. He was able to send a little money back home with regularity.

Eventually Mom joined him and they got married in early 1958, ready to start a new life away from intense racism. If only that were completely true. There were still hard and fast rules about what Blacks could do and where we could do it. We couldn't go south of 31st street without "a pass" that said we were working for someone, especially after dark. Mom did domestic work for some White families, and she had to carry a note that said she was welcomed there.

Life was tough for my parents in Kansas City in the late 1950s and early 1960s. But it was better than life in the deep south, so they didn't complain, at least to me. I'm guessing that among friends they voiced their concern, but not publicly.

There are so many families that will focus on the negatives, what you can and can't do. They focused on the opportunities that did exist. Mom, especially, encouraged us to strive to achieve beyond what others expected of us. It was important for us to go to school and work hard.

I was born in Kansas City, Missouri, on September 20, 1958. I lived in central Kansas City where diversity was the norm. People from a variety of backgrounds and races grew up together, attended school together, and, most important to me, played together. We didn't play on official teams, we just picked sides and played from early in the day until late at night. We took breaks, but only to eat lunch or dinner.

I started my education at Faxon Elementary School. Desegregation sent me to Volker Elementary School for a few years. It didn't bother me that I was being bused, because Volker was a much nicer school with better resources. Plus, most of my buddies went with me to Volker.

My parents taught us to respect others, and it didn't matter to us what color their skin was. So when there were other kids in my class who didn't look like I did it didn't matter. With all the racial strife in America at the time, we seemed to be insulated from much of it.

I'm thankful that my parents brought us up the way they did. I know a lot of guys who grew up in the same neighborhood at the same time who were angry. They saw the inequities, and instead of being a catalyst for change, they chose the more destructive path. Many of my classmates chose a path of drugs and crime. Girls in my school got pregnant before they graduated. That happened in other neighborhoods too, including White neighborhoods. But it seemed to be more prevalent in the inner-city.

But we avoided the anger and the resulting trouble. My parents were great people, but they don't get all the credit. There was one man in particular, a German guy named Hans, who probably remembered some of the rampant racism that caused Nazi Germany to grow in power. He went around the neighborhood and picked up kids to take them to church for fun activities. My Mom was happy that we were getting involved in a church, because she was a church-goer herself. Dad was not opposed to Christianity, but I don't recall him being involved much.

Hans got me involved in attending Sunday School at a Presbyterian church around third or fourth grade. I enjoyed that time, because it wasn't just sitting in a class and learning. We got to learn in a playful setting, making the Christian lifestyle appealing.

Eventually—maybe three or four years later—Mom started taking us to Palestine Baptist Church, where she attended. My Sunday School teacher, Brenda Jenkins, had a way of teaching that was very appealing. She was very loving, and she explained the Gospel in a way that I could understand. She explained to me that even if I tried as hard as I could, I could not earn salvation. I was a sinner, and I needed grace. She told me about Heaven and Hell, and that I would end up in one of those places when I died. It was up to me, because Jesus offered salvation and all I had to do was accept it.

I knew I didn't want to spend eternity in "the smoking section," so I gave my life to Christ when I was in eighth grade. It changed my life for eternity, but my life on Earth didn't change that much. I was a respectful, moral kid, so I didn't appear much different. And sports were still really important.

Don't get me wrong; I was not an angel. I should mention that my athletic focus did get me into some trouble. I was very competitive, and that manifested itself in ways that weren't always the most honorable.

I was nicknamed "Smiley" in my early years, due to my disposition. I was always smiling, and I was pretty easy-going. But when I was in fourth or fifth grade, I had a nemesis named Nathaniel. He didn't like the fact that I was always happy, and he tried to bait me into confrontations.

One time, when things got particularly heated between us, the gym teacher brought out the boxing gloves and told us go to the gym. He wanted to settle it "fair and square," or so he said. He arranged three fights, and students were charged a nickel to see each one. (I never found out who kept all the nickels, but I never saw them.)

The three fights ended up with each of us winning one and drawing the third, based on the "judge's decision." (I'm not saying it was rigged, but I believed I won at least two of the fights.) But it was a battle between "good and evil." I used to wear a shirt that said, "Frazier" on it, because I liked Joe Frazier. Unlike many of my classmates but a lot like much of the rest of America, I didn't like Muhammed Ali, due to his arrogance and brash behavior. My friends ended up calling me Frazier, because whatever I did I wanted to do it with humility. I wore my Frazier shirt in the fights against Nathaniel. Interestingly, Nathaniel always wore a shirt that said, "Ali."

The atmosphere around those fights was sort of like the Ali-Frazier "Thrilla in Manilla" heavyweight championship in the Philippines. We had huge crowds, so I'm sure that gym teacher took in quite a bit of extra change. We never had a final bout to break the tie, and we both went on to different schools for middle school. But I will always remember trying to represent the proper way to win or lose in athletics.

I stayed involved in sports, and that directed a lot of my youth.(I only did baseball on a team by the 7th grade. Football & wrestling started in 10th grade for me) I was an all-star in three different sports. Baseball was always my favorite, and I played a lot of baseball. I thought I might someday play for the Royals as a middle infielder. Our school didn't have a team, but I played on teams all summer long. My team was pretty good, but we got beat by a team from South Kansas City. The rules allowed the winning team to select a player from each of the other teams. I was chosen, and we represented Kansas City in the under-14 World Series in Knoxville, Tennessee, in 1973.

Greg (kneeling, fourth from left) was part of an all-star team that represented Kansas City in a national tournament in Tennessee.

I also wanted to play football, but my Dad missed the deadline for sign-ups. When I started my freshman year at East High School, I can't tell you why, but I didn't play football. It wasn't until 10th grade that I tried out for the football team.

I broke my arm when I hit the unpadded portion of the blocking dummy. I hit it and bruised my arm, but I was intent on impressing the coach, so I kept going after it. Eventually I couldn't take the pain and a doctor's exam showed that I broke my left forearm. I was always a little chunky, which brought some ridicule from my classmates. That got worse when I had to wear a cast. They said that I must be soft. But the center on the football team apparently liked my tenacity, because he suggested that I try out for the wrestling team that was going to start that year.

I had never had any knowledge of or interest in wrestling, so I balked.

RACE IN AMERICA: A CALL TO HEAL

But he insisted, so I tried out. My first match against a stud from Van Horn High School I got pinned in a little more than a minute. In my second match I got pinned again, but it took until the second period. My third match I didn't get pinned. I still lost, 19-9, but I saw progress. I lost my first seven matches. Finally, in a double-dual meet with Shawnee Mission West and Shawnee Mission South, I was getting destroyed by this guy from West. I was used to my opponent being on my left side, so I was off-balance when this guy chose my right side. With less than 20 seconds left I was down 8-0.

For some reason, that kid switched to my left side. I knew what to do, and with less than 10 seconds remaining, I rolled him. He was flat on his back, and if he had managed to keep his shoulders off the mat for a few more seconds, he would have won on points. But he didn't and the official hit his hand on the mat. I had pinned him for my first victory.

Greg became one of the best wrestlers in the state, despite not picking up the sport until 10th grade.

I can't describe what that was like for me. I was a good sport, so when the match was over, I always shook my opponent's hand before the referee raised his hand to signify the victory. That day, he raised *my* hand, and I was hooked! I loved that feeling—it felt like electricity going through my veins!—and it motivated me to push harder. I finished my sophomore season with a 7-11 record, but most of those losses were early in the year.

My junior year, I finished 16-3, and I lost one match short of reaching the state tournament. My senior year, I smoked practically everybody. I was 16-1, and my only loss of the season came in the second round of the state meet.

I owe a lot of the credit to Chuck Sears, a White man who was the head wrestling coach at Blue Springs High School out in the suburbs. He won several state titles there. I'm not sure where I met him, but he took an interest in this Black kid from the inner-city. He allowed me to come to work with his guys during my junior and senior years of high school.

Coach Chuck Sears was a big part of Greg's early development, and they remain close friends to this day.

RACE IN AMERICA: A CALL TO HEAL

I traveled the U.S. with his wrestlers, and I got exponentially better by learning from him. He was the type of coach who taught each guy according to what was best for him, as opposed to all guys doing the same thing. He also helped me as a coach for many years. I've considered him my mentor and I realize that my success in wrestling, especially, was due to his efforts.

I played football my last two years, and I was first-team all-conference my senior year. I got recruited to wrestle and play football at the University of Missouri, but I knew I probably wouldn't have much chance to compete at that level. I also was recruited by Central Missouri State University, and I knew that I could compete there, so I became a CMSU Mule.

My success in athletics allowed me to receive better treatment from Whites than most Black kids experienced, so I still didn't get hit with racial inequality too badly. I wrestled against kids from predominantly White schools, and was treated respectfully by my opponents and the crowds most of the time. I got to travel beyond the boundaries of Black Kansas City because of sports, and I was more well-rounded because of that.

Sports also got me introduced to the Fellowship of Christian Athletes, which helped me gain more perspective of other neighborhoods and other cultures. I also got to share my perspective with people who were sheltered from my culture. John Shore, who eventually was my boss when I worked for FCA, took me all over the area, where I spoke to FCA Huddles and business groups. It helped me develop relationships with people who have influenced my life to this day.

I'll address more of this in chapter 5 on how sports causes and can help solve problems with racial dissension, as well as the chapter on how religion does and can do the same.

I don't want to paint the picture that I didn't see the difference in Black and White. It just didn't matter to me.

Today, I can go to places like Worlds of Fun any time I want. My kids don't understand how that wasn't always the case. Before Worlds of Fun opened in the early 1970s, there was an amusement park at 75th and Prospect called Fairyland Park. It wasn't as big as Worlds of Fun, but it was the only option we had.

Well, really, we only had that option one day a year. Blacks were allowed to attend Fairyland Park on Easter Sunday. But instead of wondering why we couldn't attend 364 days out of the year, we were excited that we got to go every year on Easter Sunday. We looked forward to it.

Interestingly, it was through my growth at Palestine Baptist Church that I finally started to grasp the difference between my life and that of my fellow believers who are White. I can't tell you how many times in church I heard, "They do this in the suburbs." We all knew that meant "the White suburbs." The White churches had their way of doing things, and we had ours.

At first, I simply took it as different. Eventually, though, I started to wonder if there really was a good reason for those differences.

Chapter 2
RACIAL ISSUES

I KNEW THINGS generally were different for Black kids than they were for White kids, but I really didn't have to experience it very much until I went to college. I chose Central Missouri State University because I thought I would have a better chance of competing in wrestling and baseball at that level than I would at the Big 8 level with the University of Missouri. It was a very good decision, as I went on to win two MIAA wrestling titles, was a two-time NCAA Division II qualifier and beat wrestlers from Mizzou three times. I ended my career at No. 2 in career wins in school history. I was inducted into the school's wrestling Hall of Fame in 2012.

But it was in Warrensburg, Mo., where the reality of racial inequality hit me like a ton of bricks.

I was sixth (out of 10 guys) in the seeding for varsity at my weight class when my freshman wrestling season started. We had competitions in practice to determine who would wrestle the No. 2 guy. Whoever won that would get to wrestle the No. 1 guy, a senior captain everybody loved. I gradually worked my way up the depth chart before finally getting the chance to wrestle the top guy for the varsity spot at that weight class.

When I wrestled him I beat him, so I made the varsity as a walk-on freshman. I was 4-8 my first year, but it was a great opportunity for me. We wrestled against MU, against Nebraska and other schools at that level. We probably shouldn't have been wrestling those guys.

At CMSU, Greg got to face some of the best wrestlers in the nation, including Vadney Rinne of Missouri.

I was the only freshman who earned a spot with the varsity and wrestled against some pretty great competition. But on the first day of practice after each weekend meet, I always had to wrestle the senior captain to retain my spot. I beat him every time, but it was very draining. While most of my teammates could relax after their matches and eat whatever they wanted, I had to keep my weight down because the following Monday I had to make weight for a varsity wrestle-off.

I believe I was only one on the squad who had to defend his spot every week. I wrestled the senior captain almost a dozen times. I think it was primarily because of his loyalty to the senior leader that the coach wanted to keep giving him a chance to get his spot back. But one has to think that it might also have been because he was White and I was Black.

A couple of weeks before the conference meet, we wrestled for the varsity spot again. He ran from me, kind of a "rope a dope" technique. He wouldn't attack, and it blew my mind. He basically stalled and the coach let him do that. I never could get to him, and he beat me on points.

To win the spot, one of us had to win two of three matches. The second match, he ran from me again. This time I threw him down a couple of times, but the coach said he was off the mat so I didn't get any points. I had thrown him so many times and so hard that he collapsed after the match. They called the ambulance and they took him to the hospital with a concussion and two black eyes. He was going to have to miss two weeks, which was up right before the conference meet.

When he was cleared to wrestle, I told the coach I wanted to wrestle him again for the spot. The coach said there would be no more competitions for spots. He got to go to the conference meet, where he took second.

I was very upset about that decision and made up my mind that I would never be sub-varsity again. I would have accepted it and not thought about it as a racial incident if there weren't other things that, looking back, cause me to wonder if it was partly because of the color of my skin.

When we traveled to away meets, I always roomed with a heavyweight wrestler. He was White, but he was an outsider on the team, just like I was. We ended up becoming friends, because there were so many times that we got left out of "unofficial" team activities. We'd get to the hotel on the road and the guys on the team would talk about meeting back in the lobby to go somewhere together. When we'd get down to the lobby, the rest of the team was always gone. After a while, we figured out that they didn't want us around.

I persevered, but it made me think that I would never want any of my other teammates to be treated that way. I devoted myself more to the pursuit of wrestling excellence, and the rejection made me stronger. When something would happen, I would embrace it and deal with it. Then I would pray about it, and that allowed me to brush it off and move on.

The racism bothered me at the time, but it was later in life that I started to be offended by it. But instead of letting that offense make me bitter, it has made me more resolved to affect change.

I experienced racism in college away from the athletic fields as well. I was recruited by several fraternities on campus, both Black and White. I knew people at every one of those frats. In Lambda Chi Alpha, there were several guys I knew from FCA. There were other wrestlers there, so I felt a closer bond with those guys.

Me wanting to join Lambda Chi was a really big deal on campus. I didn't know that I would become the first Black to be a member of Lambda Chi at CMSU. I didn't even think about it. I just looked at it as an opportunity to join a fraternity that had Christian roots.

At some of the parties around campus, the other fraternities would sing derogatory songs about the Lambda Chi's accepting Blacks. I was treated very well in the fraternity, though there were still a few times I was denigrated as "the Black guy." But it definitely created some issues among other frats on campus.

I was in a sociology class and the subject of integrating the fraternities came up. They talked about a Black guy who joined the Lambda Chi's. They didn't mention my name, but they talked about how I was the first guy to break the color barrier on that campus. It was presented without any kind of bias, but it was talked about being very historical.

For the most part, the racism usually was well-concealed. There usually was something that went along with it that could be used as rationale or a defense for the bad treatment. Many knew what it was, but there was always an out.

One night during the fall of 1977, my sophomore year, I was hanging out in my dorm room with my roommate and a female friend. It was around 10:30 p.m. and I'd lost track of time, because we were just talking and listening to some "Earth, Wind and Fire." My R.A. came into the room and told us that we had broken a dorm rule, because girls weren't allowed in the guys' dorm past 10 p.m. I didn't think it'd be a big deal, because other guys in the dorm had been caught either with drugs or having sex in their rooms, and very little, if anything, was done to them.

I had to go to the Dean of Men. He was very old, and apparently he also was very old school. He told me there would be a hearing and they would try to embarrass me. Word got out, and it became much bigger than just me.

A local reporter came to my room soon to ask me about how I was discriminated against. He wrote an article about how this was unfair. I told him that I was considering transferring to another school to get away from the whole situation. He said he'd only print it if I stayed to fight it, but eventually I told him that I was going to leave.

I left CMSU to transfer to Longview Community College in Kansas City to play baseball in Spring 1978. I played baseball that spring and went to Penn Valley Community College during the summer.

As fall rolled around, I decided that I would transfer to Northwest Missouri State University or Southwest Missouri State University. I was leaning toward SMSU, but I didn't know how to get to Springfield. I knew my wrestling coach at CMSU knew, so on my way south I went by Warrensburg to get directions to SMSU. He told me about the prejudice at those schools, and talked me into staying at CMSU.

I'm glad he did, because that fall I met a very lovely young lady named Becky McCulloch. One of her good friends was one of our wrestling managers. She had dated a wrestler in high school, so she was into wrestling. She would come and watch me wrestle. Apparently she liked to watch me beat people up. I was a "lean, mean, fighting machine."

Becky was attracted to this "lean, mean, fighting machine."

Becky is White, but that didn't matter to me. I was really starting to fall in love with her. Eventually we decided that we could be happy together for the long term. We knew there would be some prejudice against us with a mixed marriage, but we thought we would be able to get past that. And besides, many marriages go through stuff anyway. So we decided to get married.

We weren't being defiant or trying to make waves; we just believed that God wanted us to be together. We were both grounded in Christ, and we felt like this was what we were supposed to do.

I remember my conversation with my Dad. He said, "You shouldn't do it." He was into politics and he looked at it from that perspective. I told him I wasn't concerned about getting "political favors" from people. I told him that Becky was perfect for me, and I couldn't imagine spending the rest of my life with anyone but her. So he said he was fine with it.

My mother was fine with it eventually, as well. She wasn't overly excited about it, growing up the way she did. But if I was sure, she would support me wholeheartedly, and she did!

Becky's parents were far less supportive. In fact, they were absolutely opposed. It was nothing personal, because we had not met. They didn't want to meet me. The fact that I am Black was a deal-killer for them.

As the wedding day approached, her parents told Becky that they would not support our marriage. In fact, they would not attend the wedding. We had to do everything ourselves, as far as wedding preparations. We found the photographer. We had a friend make our cake. Becky made her own dress.

All the things that a bride-to-be usually does with her mother, Becky had to do on her own. I tried to help as much as I could, but I know it was tough for her to not have that bonding time with her Mom.

The week of the wedding, I drove down to Warrensburg from Kansas City to help with the final plans. Becky was in summer school and already was living in married-student housing at CMSU where we would live after the wedding. Each day we worked on different plans for the Friday wedding. On Monday evening, we looked out the window and saw a couple coming up the sidewalk.

I asked Becky who they were and she told me that it was a couple from her home church of many years. This couple tried to be nice, but for about an hour they told us that there were many reasons why we shouldn't get married. They were all related to the fact that she was White and I was Black. They were polite, but not very convincing. The next day, another couple showed up. They were from Becky's home church as well. They tried different reasons, but their argument was basically the same. Becky is White and I'm Black, and that just wouldn't work.

Becky and I were in love. We believed that God wanted us to be married. We had prayed about it, and we knew that we could endure whatever came our way.

On Wednesday, another couple showed up. This time the look on Becky's face was different as she looked out the window. Again I asked her who they were, and she said, "It's my Mom and Dad." She had no idea they were coming.

Two days before the wedding and I finally was going to meet my future in-laws. The first two couples hadn't worked, so it was time to send in the "heavy artillery."

Becky's Dad came in first with a huge Bible in his hands. He shook my hand and sat down. He told me that he was not prejudiced. In fact, he told me, he had eaten with a "colored guy" once. He told me that I was welcome in his home at any time, as long as I brought along my "little colored girl."

He then opened his Bible and read a portion of 2 Corinthians 6:14. He said, "Thou shall not be unequally yoked," and then slammed his Bible shut. As a Christian, I should know that God would not approve of a mixed marriage.

I had studied Scripture too, and I told him that the whole verse says, "unequally yoked in the Spirit." That warning was meant to instruct Christians not to marry non-Christians. Opposing life-views would not allow for spiritual growth of both people. It wasn't the color of one's skin that God was warning against, but the heart and the propensity to worship false Gods.

Becky's Dad told me I was wrong. I didn't argue any further, as it seemed pointless. He went on to say he wasn't sure if or how they'd disrupt the wedding. He said they had a great concern for neighbors and family, as well as how our children would be treated. Out of the corner of my eye, I could see Becky and her Mom. Lots of tears flowed during that intense time.

They finally left, and Becky was a mess. I loved on her for a while, and we finished our plans. We made arrangements to resist anything her parents might do to disrupt things. I had a few of my buddies from football (linebackers and linemen) and wrestling as ushers, so we felt like the wedding would not be disrupted.

The wedding went great. We became Mr. and Mrs. Greg Thomas on August 8, 1980. Most of her family came. The only no-shows were her parents and her brother and sister, who were both still in high school. They wouldn't allow them to go.

**Greg's and Becky's wedding picture included Greg's parents,
but not Becky's.**

Once the wedding had happened, we thought maybe things would get better. But they didn't. Her parents didn't want anything to do with their son-in-law. It was as if the wedding never happened.

The following summer, there was a huge family reunion in Higginsville, Mo. The matriarchs of the family urged Becky and me to show up. We didn't want to be a source of conflict, so we declined. But they insisted, and we finally decided to go.

We arrived in town and went to a huge gym where the reunion was to be held. When we walked through the door, silence fell on the entire room. Becky's parents, brother and sister got up and walked right past us. There was no eye contact and no words were spoken. There was an awkward hush for a while, but we had a party after that.

There's an expression that time heals all wounds, but for us, time had no affect on the relationship, or lack of one.

For the first three Christmases of our married life, I would take Becky to her parents place near Odessa, Mo., and then had to sit in the car for the duration of her time for the family Christmas meal. After they finished exchanging presents, Becky would come out and we'd drive home.

It wasn't what I would choose, but I accepted it, because I loved her. I told myself, "You've just got to do this. She's got to be there, because they've only got X amount of years left. So she's got to be there." I thought of people who went through some really serious stuff. Me sitting out in the car was no big deal.

Becky was uncomfortable with the situation, and she finally decided to not go through it any more. She told me that if her family would not accept me they could not accept her. For the next 18 years, we went elsewhere for Christmas.

When our daughter BreAnn was born on Sept. 25, 1982, things started to change, at least with her Mom. Bre was breech so Becky had a C-Section. Becky's Mom knew it was serious, because she delivered Becky via C-Section. So she came to the hospital and waited in the waiting room.

I was back with Becky through the early stages of the delivery, but a problem forced the doctors to sedate Becky. They made me leave the room, and I paced back and forth in the hall. After Bre was born, they called me back in the room and I got to be the first person to hold her. After that, they sent me to the waiting room for recovery. That time was a bit awkward at first, because we were the only two people in that big room. We started with small talk, and as we talked she realized that I was a regular human being. We ended up getting along very well.

From that day forward, even though I was not welcome in her house (because of her husband), we connected. I would see her at various times, and I could talk with her.

Things did not change with Becky's Dad, however. Becky and our kids had to go to her parents' home in order to see them. They never came to our home, and I was not invited to join them.

But about a month after the terrorist attacks on Sept. 11, 2001, and the recognition of their 50th wedding anniversary, I got a call from her Dad asking me what we'd be doing for Thanksgiving. I have to admit that it caused me to pause. I was not expecting him to call. But I knew I had to respond in a Christian manner. So I agreed to bring our family and come to Thanksgiving dinner.

What I heard from Becky was the fact that they were celebrating their 50th wedding anniversary that year had an impact on her Dad. But it was also partly due to a sermon he heard about carrying bitterness in your heart to your grave. None of the folks who died in the terrorist attacks on 9/11 thought they were headed to work that morning to die. The pastor encouraged them to get rid of any lingering bitterness.

I don't recall what Becky's reaction was, but I have a feeling she already knew, or at least had a hunch that the invitation was coming. Regardless, she was happy, and she just smiled.

When we got to her parents' house, it was a little like the movie "Guess Who's Coming to Dinner" (the 1967 movie with Sidney Poitier).

The way I've always looked at that situation is like a wrestling match.

I've wrestled against world champions and Olympic champions. I'd go against some of the baddest dudes in the world, and I knew there was the potential that I was going to get ripped apart. This was a lot less intimidating. I went into it prepared for whatever would happen.

I really wanted this relationship to grow, for my sake and for Becky's and the kids' sake, even though it took far too long to get started. So we talked about things that would make him comfortable. We talked about his time in the Korean War and about cars. We got along fine, and we embraced when we got ready to leave. The relationship grew through the next several years. I honored him at my Dad's funeral in 2007. I also spent time with him in the three days before his death in 2008.

The fact that he attended my Dad's funeral was a really big deal. Many of the people there knew all about our past, so it made a huge impact that he was there.

Becky's Mom now is very much a part of my life. I always wondered if she felt the same way her husband did, or if she just deferred to him. She and I got along when I'd call, or when she would call our house and I answered. But she now treats me like a son and I treat her like a mom. We'll get together for lunch and discuss current events. She's very gracious and giving.

Becky and I got married before our senior year at CMSU. I finished my college career as one of the most successful wrestlers in school history. I was also a good student. There were seven seniors on the wrestling squad, and I was by far the most successful. I went to several job placement events, and I always was well-received. But for some reason, I was the only one who was not offered a coaching job before or after graduation.

Greg got used to having his arm raised in victory. He now is a part of the Central Missouri State University Wrestling Hall of Fame.

I decided to go to the head of the physical education department and ask if she thought I should be having trouble getting a job. She said that I shouldn't because of quotas. I was stunned. I didn't want to get a job *because* I was Black. I wanted to get a job because I was qualified, regardless of the fact that I was Black.

There were plenty of openings, and I had some feelers, but I never got the job. I got a chance several times, but I couldn't get the contract.

In my final semester, I did my student teaching at Lee's Summit High School. I also coached baseball and freestyle wrestling. The head wrestling coach at the time was preparing to retire, and he asked me if I would be interested in the job. I told him I was definitely interested. Word got out quickly.

RACE IN AMERICA: A CALL TO HEAL

There was a kid on the baseball team who knew a member of the school board. He came to me after practice one day. He told me that Lee's Summit and Blue Springs schools weren't ready to hire Black head coaches.

In August of 1981, three months after graduation, I had opened a business delivering auto parts to automotive garages. A rural school district east of Kansas City suddenly found itself in need of a head wrestling coach and assistant football coach. They got my resume from CMSU and couldn't believe that they still had a shot at a wrestler with my accomplishments.

I interviewed with the principal and superintendent on a Friday a couple of weeks before school started. It went great, as we knew many of the same people, including the head football coach who was my FCA Camp Huddle leader in Estes Park, Colo., the summer after my junior year of high school. They told me to bring Becky to their town two days later to look for housing. I had had to wait longer than any of my classmates, but I was finally going to get a job.

I was about as excited as I could be. When Becky and I got there that Sunday, we sat with the principal to go over class schedules and general info before I was to go meet with the football coach to go over football responsibilities. At that time, the superintendent came in, but quickly excused himself. I thought it was to use the rest room, but he told us later it was to do a phone poll of the school board members. He came back in a few minutes and pulled the contract back.

I didn't pay any attention to that, because I was so excited about my first coaching job. Becky figured it out before I did, and she started to cry. It became clear that I wasn't getting this job. The superintendent told me that it was unanimous among the board members that I wasn't to be hired. He said that if I were a math or science teacher, I would be hired on the spot. But being a coach I would be a role model. He said that I wouldn't be served in restaurants and parents would complain.

After the full weight of the decision set in, I told them that it was times like that that I remembered Romans 8:28 ("*And we know that in all things God works for the good of those who love him, who have been called according to his purpose.*"). They told me they weren't familiar with the verse, so I told them what it said.

The superintendent reached into his pocket to give me $2.50 for meal money. He told me he'd fight for me at the next board meeting, but I knew that the decision was made.

I eventually filed a complaint with EEOC and was told it would take six months to a year to investigate this case. But the following week an attorney from that district called me to set up a meeting. I was unsure what I should do, but several people told me not to accept a position. They said that I would be fired for being a minute late to class, or something else trivial, and then I would have no recourse.

This guy used fast-talking and pressure to try to intimidate me. He wanted to avoid a trial, because he knew they were wrong. He offered me $1,000 to not accept the job, and more importantly, to drop my complaint, but I didn't accept that. I knew I had a case. He went to $2,000, to $3,000 and kept going up until he got to a number I could accept.

It was all over. I had a sizable amount of money in the bank, but I still didn't have a coaching or teaching job. I was amazed that I had made the most money of my life to that point *not* to take a job.

Interestingly, about six years later, I was coaching a wrestling match against that district. A lady who was the superintendent came up to me to apologize for what they did to me before she got there.

Unfortunately, that wasn't the only time an opportunity was yanked from underneath me.

In 1993, a high school that was literally in my neighborhood needed a head wrestling coach and assistant football coach. I spoke to the principal, who had worked with me when I was student teaching. He was very excited about having me coach there. I didn't know that I would be the first Black head coach in that school district's history.

All of my interviews went great. I met with the director of personnel, and our interview went well. But later I found out that his future son-in-law was also applying for the position. He wasn't qualified, and I had about 10 years of experience.

Following our interview I heard nothing for several weeks. I kept reaching out to him. When I finally reached him, he told me that their investigation had found that I'd been in several prisons for sale and possession of heroin. I laughed when he told me this, but he sternly said "It's not funny!"

I told him that I would agree totally if that info were true. He said he'd do more investigating. This alarmed me as I thought I could be traveling to an event and get stopped by police. If this information showed up on my record, I could get hauled in for something I didn't do or know anything about.

A friend with the local police department told me there wasn't anything on my record. Finally, a police sergeant, whose kids wrestled in a nearby youth program, came to my aid. He'd seen me in action loving on kids. He felt badly that this was being done to me, so he did some more investigating. He eventually came to my house one Sunday to bring me the news that he'd found my "evil twin."

If it weren't so disgusting it would be funny. The guy who used my name as his alias and caused me so much trouble was a White guy with long blonde hair and tattoos. The sergeant took this information to the principal. Later, I contacted the director, who seemed very disappointed. He told me my contract would be sent to me by mail. I told him that I lived very close so I would come by the district office to get it.

Usually that is a bustling place with plenty of activities all the time. When I went in to sign the contract, all the office doors were closed. My contract was sitting on the middle of a table, all by itself. It looked and felt like a ghost town. I grabbed it and signed it, then I walked out. There was an eerie feeling about the whole process.

I worked for that district for a year. There were some great triumphs in that short period of time, but a few challenges hit me hard as well. I was hassled on every opportunity, it seemed, including opportunities that had to be created from nothing.

I was the defensive coordinator for the freshman team. Our third game was a road game, and I was told that the bus would leave at 2:45 p.m. I made it there about 2:30 p.m., but the bus had gone already. At first I thought it hadn't arrived and that the team must be doing some last-minute meeting. But when I asked the varsity coach about it, he said it had left.

I drove to the other school in time to help with pregame. After the game, I was the last coach to leave the locker room. The next day I was summoned to the principal's office *for failing to show up for the game*. I denied it vigorously and suggested that they ask the kids. There was no effort made to verify my story, and I was told that I was no longer coaching the freshman team. I told him the parents would wonder about me just dropping out during the season like that. It didn't matter; I was told to focus on wrestling.

This was a very bitter pill to swallow, as I was doing very well with the kids.

I also was a PE teacher at the middle school besides my coaching duties. I was given six of the most notorious kids in the school. I guess they figured that they could blame me if those kids acted up.

One day, the motor to close the door that separated the girls and boys gyms had a malfunction. It wouldn't close completely. There was about a 10-inch split that allowed the girls to stick their heads in the gap and disrupt our class with catcalls—and vice versa. I was written up for a "class disruption" I told them that I couldn't fix the door. In fact, it was a few days before it was fixed by maintenance, but the write-up stayed on my record.

Finally, in the Spring, one of my notorious kids (a Black one) attacked another kid (a White one). He just started hitting this mild-mannered kid for no apparent reason. I pulled them apart, but when I looked back at the activity in the class in front of me, he went back at him. I finally took the crying kid to the office to let him know he'd done nothing wrong.

I was told to go home to take a few days off while they investigated the incident. A few weeks later I was called to a meeting with the personnel director, and he told me I couldn't coach there any more. He said "Boy (in *that* way), we'd hoped you'd be the best thing since sliced bread, but it didn't work." He went on to say, "Don't worry we'll send you some money."

We had a very good wrestling season with lots of potential to become a power in the Midwest. For much of the season, we were ranked No. 1 in the local paper. Some parents recognized that a lot of the success was because of coaching, and they went to bat for me. The night of the school board meeting, the parents lined the road in front of the district building. The local television stations came to the board meeting and at another time to my middle school to ask the principal why I was treated the way I was.

There was plenty of attention focused on my situation, but it just dragged out. Eventually, some of my wrestlers transferred to other schools to help build their programs. Even if I had gotten my job back, the turmoil had broken up our team. This was very disheartening for families, as we'd developed a huge wrestling club that was on the move. Not only was the focus on wrestling excellence, but academic and community success were key components. I've always felt that the most important thing a wrestling coach can teach his squad is to honor Christ in all they do. This will lead to great success as a student, athlete, husband and dad.

My year at that district lasted a lot longer in my life. A few years later I was the plaintiff in a Federal lawsuit as the district had broken four federal statutes in the process. I had no idea, but a few caring teachers told me about those statutes.

After about two years of delays and extensions, they asked my attorney if I would be interested in settling out of court for a nice sum. Before making a final offer, they decided to check out the jury pool. They were mostly older White men and women, so they decided to take a chance in a trial with that demographic. It was an ingenious move, as the jury didn't feel that racism still existed and the proof wasn't enough. It was amazing to me that the jury believed the testimony that racism had ended in the United States in the 1930s and 1940s.

Immediately after the verdict was read, I saw the one Black person on the jury walking toward the parking lot. I stopped him and asked him what had happened. He said that several of the jurors knew that the district had not treated me fairly, but they couldn't sway the older members of the jury to go along with their decision. In the end, they all just wanted to get on with their lives, so they voted "not guilty."

There were plenty of other examples of "coincidences" that painted me in a negative light. Were they because I was Black? I can't say for sure, but I believe some of them were. I'm like any other coach or teacher. I'm not perfect and never will be. It has usually seemed that I've been held to a different standard. It has seemed that I've generally had to find a place where they were desperate for a coach just to get a shot.

At one teaching job, my principal came by to do an evaluation of my class. He got there about three minutes before the bell. I asked him if I could hit the restroom quickly since he was there. He said to go ahead. When my evaluation was done, he'd written me up for being late to class.

At another school, I was a para. All of us were asked to write down the areas in which we were strongest, so we could help the kids. I put down history, physical education and algebra. There was a great need in a biology class, so, for the team I said I'd do it. When evaluation came in my supervisor wrote me up for lack of knowledge of subject matter. I reminded her that biology wasn't a class I wanted and that I was only there due to a great need. That evaluation stayed in my record.

The rest of this book could be about all the things I experienced because I'm Black. But I want this book to be about solutions, not just problems. In the next chapter, we'll discuss the root of the problem. If we don't know—or at least have a pretty good idea of—the cause of the problems, there's no way we can lay out potential solutions.

Chapter 3
ROOT OF THE PROBLEM

RACISM STILL EXISTS. It might be better than it was 150 years ago, and it might be better than it was 50 years ago. But it still exists, and will continue to exist, as long as we have the attitude that we are better than someone else.

It's not a skin-color issue. It's not an economic issue. It's not a geographic issue. A lot of those things may enter into the equation, but they're not the root of the problem. The urban versus suburban divide may be caused by racism, but it doesn't cause racism. In my 35 years of experience as a teacher and a coach, I've been in many different types of settings, and I've encountered many different types of kids in those settings.

Kids, like adults, have a tendency to relate according to those people around them—their teachers, coaches, teammates or classmates—not strictly from a racial standpoint. A White kid who lives in the 'Hood will tend to act like other kids in the 'Hood. He might wear his pants sagging or be able to do the "Whip" or the "NaeNae" or those types of things.

Black kids who live out in the country tend to know more about country music, or wear boots and a cowboy hat. I was in an inner-city school once and heard two White kids calling each other "nigga." It wasn't in a demeaning way; it was more like "dude." They were probably fourth or fifth grade, and that was the culture they were in. That was very eye-opening to me, because I hadn't heard that before.

The Black vs. White divide is the most obvious, because it's so visible. But the economic differences are just as real. Again, those differences are caused *by* attitude toward others, not the other way around.

So if it's not any of those issues that cause racism at its core, what is it? It's an issue of the heart, plain and simple. If you think you're better than me, or if I think I'm better than you, that's a problem. Let's call it what it is. It's a *sin issue* that manifests itself in racism in America.

It's not a recent phenomenon. The most profound aspect of this attitude is slavery in America. If you enslave a person and take away his or her freedom, it's because you think they're less valuable as a person than you. In fact, slavery was rationalized by religious groups early in our nation's history by devaluing Blacks as "less than human." The prominent attitude was that Blacks didn't deserve their freedom.

It goes back even further than that. The way our country's settlers treated the Indians (Native Americans) was predicated on the fact that they didn't "deserve" to occupy all the land that the settlers wanted.

Our country is called a "melting pot," because of all the different ethnic groups that have settled here. But very few of those groups were not discriminated against at some point, usually when they first arrived. The ethnic group in power looked down on the other groups, which is another way of saying "I'm better than you."

A lot of those situations have an economic theme to them, especially with industry and a necessary work-force. With the industrial revolution, there was a greater need for a ready and affordable work-force. Work conditions rarely were ideal, and if the owners viewed the employees as equals, there would be no way to subject them to those conditions. However, if the work-force was viewed as "lesser human," or, worse yet, as "less than human," it was easier to justify.

There are plenty of examples around the world and throughout history where this attitude has created unfair and merciless treatment of groups of people. But we're going to focus on America.

What's unique in American history is how Black people were treated—as a whole—for more than 200 years by their White neighbors. It's called "chattel slavery," where people were brought from another country, stripped of everything they know and own, including their dignity, and then sold as property. This is different from slavery known in almost every culture, including in Bible times.

People could sell themselves into slavery, but they were still a person. More importantly, they had the right to be redeemed, by working for a period of time or by being purchased by someone else for the sake of giving them freedom. Sometimes slavery was a punishment for incurring a debt that one could not pay. But that was still a result of something the person did, not something outside of their control, like the color of their skin.

In America from the mid-1600s to the mid 1800s, slavery was much worse that at any point in any country in history. Slaves were so deval-ued that it was commonly accepted that they could be raped, beaten (to death, if necessary, because of the Casual Killing Act of 1669), and worked ridiculous hours and under ridiculous conditions for the ben-efit of the slave owner. Slaves were not allowed to get an education. They could not speak with Whites unless spoken to. They had no rights whatsoever (unlike many examples of slavery in world history).

This is a point where racism became an easy manifestation of the heart issue. With Blacks in a White culture, it was easier to segment them because it took no effort to identify them. Where a group of people from Germany, for example, might blend into a society of Irish or Italian people, Blacks could not blend in because of the color of their skin.

Let's make a huge distinction here. It's not because Blacks were any different on the inside, but Whites could easily identify them, and then rationalize their behavior. That's where the issue of the heart—or sin—enters into the equation.

If we agree with what the Bible says about the human race—that we are created in the image of God—it doesn't matter what you look like. If you look at someone in any way less than you, that's a sin. I believe in the inerrant nature of the Bible, so I believe with all my being that this is true.

Look at Galatians 3:26-28: "So in Christ Jesus you are all children of God through faith, for all of you who were baptized into Christ have clothed yourselves with Christ. There is neither Jew nor Gentile, neither slave nor free, nor is there male and female, for you are all one in Christ Jesus." This verse clearly states that there is no difference between any of us.

It's interesting to note that as divided as our country is now, culture was far more about "haves and have-nots" during this period of time. The Apostle Paul was writing to a church immersed in the difference between Jew and non-Jew. They absolutely looked at the other as less-than themselves, and their culture and belief system said they couldn't even associate with each other. Slave or free had huge significance for obvious reasons. Even males and females had different rights and privileges, and who can choose if they're born male or female?

Paul was telling these people that they need to put those differences aside.

But even if you don't believe that the Bible is the ultimate source of wisdom and truth, look at some of the documents that are part of our nation's foundation. The second paragraph of the United States Declaration of Independence says, "We hold these truths to be self-evident, that all men are created equal, that they are endowed by their Creator with certain unalienable Rights, that among these are Life, Liberty and the Pursuit of Happiness." Tell me where it says "all White men." It doesn't, but that's how it was interpreted by White slave owners.

Jim Wallis talks about this in his book, "America's Original Sin." When our nation was formed, our "original sin" was in the way we treated Blacks and Indians. The country was built on a fault-line. In 1776—and in 1876 and even in 1976—we weren't all created equal. There was a difference. We need to acknowledge that. We still live in denial.

Interestingly, there is a theory that the Blacks were chosen, not because the Whites thought they were "less human," but because they were easily identified and there was an almost unlimited supply of "harvest-able goods." The "less human" status was a way to justify the inhuman treatment. It's called "cognitive dissonance." When people know what they're doing is wrong, they must come up with a theory to justify their actions.

This is strictly an unprovable theory, because there is no way to know if it's true.

What is pretty much accepted is the fact that the South was opposed to the abolition of slavery because of economics. The invention of the cotton gin in 1793 made the production of cotton big business, and slavery made the picking of cotton much more economical. Giving up the cheap labor cut deeply into profits. By the time President Abraham

Lincoln "freed the slaves" in 1863*, the economy of cotton was too entrenched in the South to abandon it. Choosing to believe that Blacks were "less human" allowed White slave owners to go to church and praise God for His blessings.

(*The Emancipation Proclamation was only symbolic. The Union states already were against slavery. The Confederate states did not recognize Lincoln's authority. While Lincoln's intent was noble, it was ineffective because it fell on deaf ears.)

That is why many people to this day don't want to have anything to do with Christianity. What kind of religious institution could condone this type of behavior. It's like Nazi Germany. Plenty of Christians knew what Adolph Hitler was doing was wrong, but they didn't want to stand up to him. They wanted to be "good Christians," obedient to the leader of their country.

The fact is, race is an easy cop-out. If you look at somebody as less than you in any way, that's a sin. Race in America has been a social construct. People weren't known as White in the country they came from. It was not until they came to America that the difference in skin-color became an issue.

A White friend recently told me that he believes most Whites cringe when they hear the term "White Supremacy" or "White Supremacist." But when we treat somebody, whether they're from a different race or not, as less valuable than ourselves, then we're doing the same thing. We're saying "we're superior to you in some way."

Everyone has different life stories. We all have different experiences. That's what makes us unique. But it doesn't make one person better than another.

Let's take a brief look at things in our nation's history that point to the fact that Blacks were treated as "less than human." This is not to point a finger of guilt. It's to highlight that it was not just an issue of disliking someone who is different. It's a matter of demeaning and devaluing an entire race of people for no other reason than the color of their skin.

The Middle Passage. This was how a large percentage of Blacks were brought to America, to be sold into slavery. They came on trade ships from Africa. They were dropped off in America, and those ships would take shipments of goods to be taken to Europe.

The Blacks were treated as cargo, nothing more than "stuff." In the process, a large percentage of the "crop" didn't make it. They would get sick and would be dumped in the ocean. The Blacks were expendable. The people in charge of the shipment didn't want to waste the money or effort to take care of them, so they would be pushed overboard. The sharks had a frenzy.

Much of White America's ancestry came into this country through Ellis Island (in New York). They came voluntarily to pursue a better life. They didn't get a whole lot of benefits. They had to work hard for what they got. But they were here because they wanted to be. They were willing to put forth the effort because there was a possible return.

A majority of Blacks, however, didn't come voluntarily, and they didn't come through Ellis Island. They came to the coastal communities in the South, in shackles. That's a huge difference. They were sold to the highest bidder. Instead of working for someone they could count on to achieve better things, they worked for people who devalued them and treated them inhumanely. Blacks didn't have the option of working hard to advance.

Another change that is not well-known is the change in how slaves "earned" their freedom. Originally (back in the 1600s), slaves could work to earn their freedom. Eventually, that changed. The cheap labor that was represented by slavery was too valuable to give it away after seven years. So slaves were slaves for life, including their offspring. They were strictly property to be owned, sold and traded. Nothing more.

Three-Fifths Compromise. The number of representatives in the House of Representatives has always been determined by how many people live in an area. People in the South wanted to count the Blacks as members of their households, so they would have a larger representation in the House of Representatives.

But since the slaves were "less than human," there needed to be a formula. The three-fifths compromise counted five slaves as the equivalent as three humans. In other words, slaves (Blacks) were worth three-fifths of a human being.

One Drop Rule. If you had any ancestor who was Black—if you had one drop of Black blood in your system—you were considered Black. My granddaughter doesn't look Black at all. She has long, blonde hair. But she's one-quarter Black, and if she were born 150 years ago, she would have no rights as a White girl.

Recently, Greg and his oldest granddaughter got to visit the Martin Luther King Jr. Memorial in Washington, D.C.

Many fair-skinned Blacks were treated better than their darker-skinned fellow slaves. They were allowed to work in the house while the Blacks were worked mercilessly in the fields. This caused dissension, even among Blacks. The Blacks who were treated worse did not like the fact that some were treated better.

But the fact is, that even the fair-skinned Blacks still lacked one essential: freedom. They could not leave their life of slavery. They still were the possession of their White owners. If a fair-skinned Black woman was attractive, there was nothing that prevented her from being raped or mistreated. If they complained or resisted, they were sent back to the field, or worse yet, beaten or killed.

Reconstruction. Once the Civil War ended, the abolition of slavery, which was completely theoretical before, became law. Blacks were free to go where they wanted and do what they wanted, according to the laws. Under President Ulysses S. Grant (two Presidents after Lincoln) laws were enacted opening various jobs to Blacks. There were Congressmen, even professional baseball players. But President Rutherford B. Hayes took away all the rights that had been given to Blacks.

From an economic standpoint, they were an uneducated, untrained work-force, only skilled in picking cotton and other trades that were associated with that, like carpenters and blacksmiths. The only places where they could use those skills were the plantations, owned by the very people they wanted to get away from.

And while they could no longer be owned, no amount of legislation changed the attitude of the White plantation owners toward their former slaves. They still viewed them as "less than human," and the working conditions and pay for work reflected that.

They had the "freedom" to look for work elsewhere, but they had no available transportation. The reality was that they really were stuck in pretty much the same situations they always had. They couldn't read or write, and even with emancipation, there was still no one who wanted to teach them.

Jim Crow. Jim Crow laws were written and unwritten rules that prohibited Blacks from having the same rights as Whites. While most think that Jackie Robinson broke the color barrier in Major League Baseball, it is more accurate to say that he "re-broke" it. Moses Fleetwood Walker and his younger brother, Weldy Wilberforce Walker, played for the Toledo Blue Stockings in the American Association, which became a major league that season. He played in 42 games and his brother played in five.

But Baseball Hall of Famer Cap Anson, who was then the manager of the Chicago White Stockings, refused to let his team play against a team with a Black player. Walker was receiving death threats, and the Blue Stockings did not bring either of the Walkers back. The color line was drawn, and for the next 63 years no one dared cross it.

It was an economic decision as well as a racial decision. If jobs were available to Blacks, some Whites would be excluded. Controlling the purse strings of nearly every money-making business, Whites controlled who could be hired and who couldn't.

This also created an interesting dichotomy. Whites believed they were superior to Blacks, but the fear of losing jobs to Blacks who were better or more qualified in a particular skill may have created the need to discriminate. Isn't it ironic that one sin (feeling that you're better than someone else) led to another (jealousy and/or envy)?

Jim Crow laws also led to separate seating on trains and buses, separate restaurants, separate water fountains, and Blacks only being allowed to go to amusement parks like Fairyland Park one day a year.

I heard once that Billy Graham got into a lot of hot water in the late 1950s for removing the rope that separated Blacks and Whites attending one of his revivals. Christians, while trying to carry out the Great Commission, were as guilty as anyone in not treating Blacks and Whites as equals. Our country was so steeped in the divide that even great preachers like Graham got into trouble for praying with Black preachers like Rev. Dr. Martin Luther King, Jr.

Convict Leasing. Following the Civil War, Blacks were repeatedly put in jail for petty crimes like vagrancy and spitting in public, in order to lease them back to plantation owners. The "convict" got nothing, because he was property of the state. The states made quite a bit of money. They weren't focusing on murderers or bank robbers. They would intentionally pick up guys who could be leased out. This practice was increased during harvest time, when there was more work than the plantation owners could handle.

The Ku Klux Klan. The KKK was founded after slavery to "save our country." There have actually been three incarnations, beginning in the 1860s. It lasted about 10 years. The second version came about in the 1920s, and the primary focus was the growing Jewish population. It lasted until 1944.

The current KKK was formed two years later, and it returned to its roots of White Supremacy. Its known membership is less than 10,000, but there are many people around the country that adhere to the beliefs espoused by the Klan.

The Klan gets a lot of the publicity, but there are plenty of groups like the KKK. They might say "We're not the KKK," but their goals are the same or very similar. They all trace their values on the fact that one race is better inherently than another. Since Sept. 11, 2001, these groups have been on the rise in America.

Civil Rights. The Civil Rights movement started in earnest right after World War II. When Jackie Robinson came back from the war, he immediately started to object to the way Blacks were treated. He made note of the fact that Blacks and Whites fought in the Armed Forces for the same rights, yet they were denied the same rights when they got back home.

Jackie played in the Negro Baseball Leagues with the Kansas City Monarchs. He objected whenever he could to the segregated treatment. One notable occasion came when the Monarch's team bus stopped to get gas. The bus had a huge gasoline tank, and the owner of the station knew who the Monarchs were. Whether it was the economics of filling that tank with gasoline, or the recognition of the team, he gladly put the hose into the tank. Robinson asked where the restrooms were. The station owner told him that the only restroom was for Whites only, and the Monarchs would have to "go out back." Robinson told him to take the hose out of the bus.

It took tremendous courage for Robinson to do that, and that courage was one of the reasons that Branch Rickey chose Robinson to cross the color barrier in 1947.

Civil rights is a name given to almost every movement that involved race relations, including the Freedom Marches in the South throughout the 1950s and 1960s; Brown vs. the Topeka Board of Education in 1954; Rosa Parks and her defiant refusal to move to the back of the bus in Montgomery, Ala. in 1955; and the "Little Rock 9" in 1957.

Over the years, Greg has had the opportunity to speak at many sites that previously saw civil unrest. His message is gradually being more accepted.

It gained momentum when a young preacher was approached about lending his support to the movement. Dr. King resisted at first, saying that he was a pastor not an activist. But when he got involved, he went at it with all his vigor. He withstood pressure from all sides, including death threats. Pastors from the North stood by him, and many of them suffered persecution because of that.

Dr. King and other leaders would train students in how to deal with racism. They would tell the students that they would have to take the abuse without fighting back. Those who agreed to passive resistance were sent to places where racism was most rampant. One group, sponsored by the Student Nonviolent Coordinating Committee, went to a diner in Fayetteville, N.C. and said they would not leave until they were served.

They were told that they would be subjected to many kinds of abuse, possibly even killed. But they had to resist fighting back. They sacrificed a lot.

Mass Incarceration. It's the new Jim Crow. There are more Blacks in prison today than there were enslaved during the 1850s. The numbers are higher partly because of a much larger population. But the "war on drugs" that was coined by President Richard Nixon in 1971 has resulted in an inordinate number of Blacks in prison.

Some will say that if they're breaking the law they deserve to be in prison. But the focus on enforcing the drug laws is on the inner-city. There are plenty of drugs in the suburbs, but way more attention is on the problem where more Blacks live. And sentences for similar crimes differ greatly between Blacks and Whites.

In the summer of 2016, two different student-athletes at Division I schools were convicted of raping unconscious women. The White student-athlete was sentenced to a sentence of three to six months. The Black student-athlete was sentenced to 15 to 25 years. There may be differences in the crimes, but there are way more similarities. The biggest difference is the penalty.

I have worked in corrections, and I've been at the juvenile detention center when kids who have been arrested are brought into the station. Far too often, the White kids are there for less time than Black kids.

While all these situations are true, I said at the beginning of this chapter that it was not a White vs. Black issue. It's a sin issue. When I think of civil rights movement in the 1960s, it was focused around the church. Dr. King, Reverend Abernathy, and the others were teaching Scripture to lead our country away from racism.

Blacks were able to vote, to go to school, etc., because of activism that started in the church. Nowadays, we've gotten away from the role of the church in race-relations. Sin has crept in, in our whole society, not just race-relations. That's a huge thing. In the 1960s, the average Black family had a mom and a dad watching the kids throughout their young lives. Nowadays, around 70 percent of Black families don't have a dad around. That puts a lot of stress on the moms. And that keeps perpetuating itself.

One final point about this. If the KKK killed as many Blacks in the inner-cities of Chicago, Detroit or Kansas City as are killed by Blacks, the media would be all over it. But the fact that it's Black on Black crime, the prevailing thought is that "they're doing it to themselves." It's more of the "they're not worth the effort to put an end to it" attitude.

That's where some of the attitude behind "Black Lives Matter" comes from. Many Whites, my White friends tell me, wonder where the "White Lives Matter" signs are. One of the key points behind that movement is that too many Blacks have been killed unnecessarily. We'll talk more about this movement in later chapters, because many of the Blacks behind it don't take into consideration that many of the victims put themselves in harm's way by decisions they made.

But the fact is, "All Lives Matter," including the unborn. In our next chapter, we'll unpack where we go from here.

If we get it right, we're on our way.

Chapter 4

SOLUTIONS

WE'VE SPENT THE first three chapters reminding you that racism still exists in America. It's certainly better than it was 150 years ago, and it's better than it was 50 years ago. It's even safe to say that it's better than it was five and 10 years ago.

But anyone who says that it no longer exists is not in touch with reality. It's not a small segment of society that still holds a grudge, and it's not a small segment of society that thinks it's much ado about nothing. It's very real and still very much a problem.

But I don't want to—or need to—spend more time on illustrating that. It's time to stop blaming each other and time to start working together. We'll never start improving until we stop irritating each other. It's time to focus on solutions—how we can start the change.

The problem didn't just start yesterday. There are several hundred years of history that got us to this point. It's been a slow process both the problem and the solution. I think a lot of younger people don't know about the history. They know about slavery, and then Abraham Lincoln freed the slaves, and then there was a problem with Civil Rights. But then Jackie Robinson broke the color barrier and, boom, everything's good.

We have a Black president and most people—Black and White—like LeBron James and Tiger Woods, so it's now an old topic. But all the things that are set up as systematic things in our country, like education system, employment and economic differences, and drastically different incarceration statistics are things we've never fully dealt with. If we can deal with those, we're on our way.

We can't deal with them in a couple of weeks. It's going to take time, just like it took a long time to establish the patterns of racism. It has to be a grass roots effort, with how you treat people on an individual basis. It can't be legislated, because a lot of people don't trust the government—on both sides of the aisle.

One great example is what was started in Dallas with the "Adopt a School" initiative through Dr. Tony Evans. It intentionally helps schools with a large percentage of at-risk kids. It's not necessarily a racial issue, but it falls into those categories because of the economic divide caused partially by racism. The at-risk kids are not at risk because they're Black or Hispanic, but because they live in areas that are more prone to problems. It's harder for those kids to "pull themselves up by their bootstraps" on their own, because the problems are systematic and inherent in their culture.

We now must do something to help them to get out. A lot of organizations will try to bring in new programs to help, but I think the kids come to school in a broken state. Many of them have "father wounds." If efforts were put toward the family, if the kids feel like they have support, we would see tremendous improvement.

In my 35-plus years as a coach and teacher, I've seen too many situations where kids come to school damaged. They came to school unprepared to learn, because they were so devastated by what they've seen and experienced at home. They don't even have a desire to learn because they don't feel that education is going to benefit them in their lives. They become disruptive at school, because it's the only way they know how to be.

When they're told to do something, many times the teacher doesn't realize what the kid is going through. If you don't know where you're going to sleep tonight, or where you're going to live next week, if things are crumbling around you, it's hard to focus on the things in class, especially if you don't see how it's going to help you. We'll discuss this phenomenon in a couple of chapters, but there are things outside of school that can be done to help.

If parents, and other adults who have an influence in the lives of young people, start making the effort to teach kids to respect teachers, police officers, military personnel, adults in general, the kids will get along better in school and in society in general. I don't see enough evidence that it's being taught.

That's a big generalization, because I know that it is being done. But it's not being done enough. Too many kids go out to face the world mad, with a chip on their shoulders. My suggestion would be for adults to teach kids from an early age, to respect authority. The teacher is there to help you, not harm you. A vast majority of teachers get into teaching because they want to love, serve and teach kids. If the kid goes to school with the thought of learning, being prepared to learn, they'll do what the teacher says and benefit from that.

Too many times, kids will not only be unprepared, they'll be disruptive, which does not create a learning environment for anyone. Teachers have to spend too much time correcting and disciplining and not enough time teaching. In those situations, kids who really want to learn may be able to learn some, but generally they can't thrive.

I believe in the truth of Proverbs 22:6, which states, "Start children off on the way they should go, and even when they are old they will not turn from it." If we teach our children from the very beginning to respect authorities, they will be far more likely to act that way when they get older. I've been around enough good schools where that is the case. I see kids who are there to learn. They come to class. They do their homework. They do what the teacher says.

So how do we start to make this change? It comes with a perception change. We must have empathy for others' needs and feelings. We must acknowledge where they are, even if we don't agree or really even understand. No one shares all the same experiences in life. We'll never know everything a person has gone through, or more importantly, is going through. If we empathize with them, recognizing the fact that these kids may be having difficulty respecting adults because all the adults in their lives have let them down, we can get to the root of the problem.

Black people, especially those raised a generation or two ago, may remember being mistreated by police for no other reason than the color of their skin. It wasn't too far in our past that the authorities didn't need an excuse to beat up a Black person. With that in the back of their mind, when they see a police officer beating—or shooting—a Black man, the first thing that comes to mind might be "Here we go again."

Greg still has the same dream as Dr. King: equality for all.

RACE IN AMERICA: A CALL TO HEAL

It's not much different than if a Jew in Germany in the 1950s or 1960s would be suspicious if they saw a police officer beating a fellow Jew. Would the first thought be, "I wonder what that person did to deserve that."? Probably not.

This does not excuse a Black man who is shot by police for resisting arrest and pulling a gun after committing a crime. Most police officers are committed to upholding the law and arresting those who violate it. Too many protests are based on the fact that the "victim" is Black and the officer who shot him is White.

But if we dig deeply enough to understand the attitudes of everyone involved, we'll have some common ground on which to build. And as effective as understanding will be, there is one more thing that will solve even more differences.

It may be the most important point in this entire book.

If we see each other the way God sees us, it will be nearly impossible to treat each other without respect. Genesis 1:27 says, "So God created mankind in his own image, in the image of God he created them; male and female he created them." We are created *in the image of God.*

Does that mean that God is Black, White, Asian or some other ethnic group? No, it means that human beings are like God in appearance. No two humans look exactly the same, but we all look like humans.

Think about this: if you encounter someone who looks just like your best friend, aren't you going to be inclined to treat them differently than if they look like someone you don't like? They aren't that other person, but there's an image in your mind that affects your perception.

This works, even if you don't believe the Bible to be the infallible Word of God. If you see the other person as a valuable part of society with similar goals and aspirations, your attitude toward them will change. You'll want to honor and respect them, even serve them, not rob from them or cause them harm.

If you look at that person as a valued person, just as valued as you are, in God's eyes, you wouldn't be so quick to judge, to disrespect, to harm or to hate. If you look at that person as having the likeness of the Creator of the universe, how can you possibly treat them with anything but respect? How can you possibly not work harder to put yourself in their shoes? When that happens, perception changes and suddenly the other person is not an adversary. You can become an advocate.

This also allows us to embrace the differences. We are created in the image of God. But just as my kids may look like me, they still have their own identity. They still have their own characteristics that make them who they are. When we accept that and move from there, we have a chance. We have a starting point. We are both created in the image of God, so we have something significant in common. How can we grow from that? How we can take that premise, recognizing that we're more similar than we are different, and manifest that in the way we treat each other.

We should not ignore the differences. We should embrace them and start singing off the same sheet of music. And when we recognize that we all have unique experiences and perspectives, we can sing off that same sheet of music, but singing harmony, not unison. We all have our gifts and we all have our roles. We all have our parts to sing, and when we're singing together we can make beautiful music.

This is not a short-term fix. We can't try it for a few months and then look to the next solution. This has to be a long-term commitment. Galatians 6:9 says, "Let us not become weary in doing good, for at the proper time we will reap a harvest if we do not give up." We have to persevere. Because there are those who want us to be at odds and they will not give up either.

If someone gets a public voice and has the audacity to say, "People of different races should be treated differently," or, "Black people are inferior (or superior) to Whites," no one would take them seriously. But the adversary will be subtle. He will attack us in clandestine ways, ways that will make sense to us unless we dig deeply enough.

Ephesians 6:12 (King James Version) states it this way: "For we wrestle not against flesh and blood, but against principalities, against powers, against the rulers of the darkness of this world, against spiritual wickedness in high places."

This is a spiritual battle. Where God wants us to treat each other with honor and respect, Satan seeks to pit us against each other. And we are easy marks. Romans 3:23 says about us, "for all have sinned and fall short of the glory of God."

This is one of the most misquoted verses in the Bible. Many people say, "for all have sinned and fallen short...," implying that once we receive salvation through Christ we stop sinning. That's not the case. There's a big difference between fallen and fall. We keep on sinning, which requires forgiveness. We must continue to accept God's grace.

How does that impact us? We must continue to grant grace to others when they fail us. If we view our fellow humans as God's likeness, then extend them grace when they fail us, we'll all get along better.

So many people want to focus on the faults of others. For some, it makes them feel better about themselves. But if we recognize our sinfulness, and look at others as "created in the image of God," the issues that divide us will melt away.

How does this look in real life? We get to know each other more than just on the surface. We invest in each others' lives and try to look at life from their perspectives. For example, a teacher with a problem student could find out the situation at home for that student, and then adjust the teaching path accordingly. That can make a huge difference in that kid's life for years to come.

There was a story told during the 2016 Little League World Series about a group of people who did just that. The Buczek Little League in Washington Heights serves one of the roughest neighborhoods in New York. It's named after Michael Buczek, a fallen New York City police officer. The kids wear the names of other officers killed in the line of duty on the backs of their jerseys.

Buczek was shot and killed in the line of duty working in Washington Heights in 1988. Following the events of September 11, 2001, the league began a tradition where every team is named after a fallen member of the NYPD. Players proudly wear the officer's name on the back of their jerseys, as well as keeping a picture of the officer in their dugout for each game.

The league has grown in size to nearly 30 teams and has seen more than 8,000 players participate. Around 35 former players have gone on to become members of the NYPD themselves. The motto of the league is, "Building Major League Citizens, One Game at a Time."

The coaches all are members of the NYPD, so the impact is not just the name on the shirts. It's personal, face-to-face. The kids of all colors can see that police officers of all colors are on their side. The impact is long-lasting.

That's a great example of investing in the lives of kids. The kids who play in this Little League have an appreciation for the police officers in their crime-ridden neighborhood that never would have been possible without that investment of time and energy.

But there are plenty of ways to make a difference that won't generate headlines. For 35 years as a coach, I've taken kids from all over the country to other parts of the country to experience different cultures. We go to compete, but they learn far more than just how to win a wrestling match or a football game. They learn how to interact with people different than they are. I still keep in contact with many of my former athletes. I know what's going on in their lives, and they know what's going on in mine. I invested myself in them.

Greg has taken kids of all sizes, shapes and colors to FCA camps, with the goal of sharing Christ's love.

I don't share this to toot my own horn. It's just an example of what can be done. It's what was done for me when I was in high school. Coach Sears invested in me, and he has impacted me for a lifetime.

You don't have to travel or expend a lot of money. Bringing kids from the suburbs to the inner-city (and vice-versa) to interact with other kids. Mentoring and just getting to know each other within the safe boundaries of education can lead to the disintegration of barriers later in life. Remember the old expression, "You only get one chance to make a first impression." We can change those first impressions for future generations.

It's already being done, but it needs to happen more. There are churches all over the United States that are intentionally getting people from different cultures together to get to know each other. You've heard of some of them, but there are plenty that you haven't heard about. But for every Matt Chandler at the Village Church in Flower Mound, Texas, there are 20 other opportunities that aren't being met.

It might be uncomfortable at first, but it's worth the effort. We can't give up, just because it's hard. There will always be those who will resist. We can't let them affect our resolve to affect change.

How can *you* play a role? Each one of us can make a difference in our own circles. Involve your kids and their friends in events or activities. Let them lead. I've seen way more times than I can count how leadership responsibilities can change the attitude of young people. Instead of being led by an adult they may or may not respect, when kids know it depends on them they will look for help wherever they can get it, including their peers they never met before.

And we can learn from the kids. If we go out of our way to meet and get to know others from outside our circle of influence, it will help. If we show an interest to hear the other person's heart, (and maybe even empathize with what they've seen or done), it also will help. We can make a difference.

I spoke at a college event recently. After hearing me speak, a student asked me if the racial climate will get better or worse in the future. I thought for a moment, and then told him, "both." We'll have a great group of people who are doing their best to love and serve others. There will also be a group who are very polarized & will continue to promote negativity.

Which side are you on?

Chapter 5

SPORTS

The year was 1963, and the Civil Rights movement was in full force. The battle lines of the movement were drawn and there was very little gray area in between. Blacks and Whites did not associate with each other very often, other than confrontations. Especially in the deep South, everyone seemed to be okay with that. But a courageous university president, athletic director and men's basketball coach set out to change the rules.

That Spring, Mississippi State University won its fourth Southeastern Conference men's basketball championship in five years. The three previous times (1959, 1961 and 1962), they declined an invitation to play in the NCAA tournament, a decision that was widely popular in Mississippi and around the South. Newspaper columnists supported the "preservation" of the unwritten law prohibiting state-supported schools from playing teams with players of another race.

But Dean Colvard, the MSU president who arrived on campus in the fall of 1960, decided it was time to change that decision. He didn't rock the boat his first year, thinking he didn't have enough clout to force change. The same was true in 1962, his second year. But he determined that if he went along with the consensus again in 1963, two things would happen. First, he would miss out on a great opportunity, maybe the last one in a long time, because the 1963 team was senior-laden.

He also would be perceived as agreeing with the unwritten law if he didn't act then. This law was true for all-White schools, like Mississippi State, and all-Black schools like Jackson State, which turned down an invitation to play in the NAIA (small schools) tournament in Kansas City in 1957 because there were schools with White players on the roster.

In 1991, Colvard was quoted as saying, "If I did not have enough of a following (on campus) to do it then, I probably never would have. And I might not have the opportunity again."

So Colvard, along with his athletic director, Wade Walker, and basketball coach Babe McCarthy decided it was time. On March 2, 1963, they announced that Mississippi State would accept the invitation. The reaction was swift and negative. Newspaper columnists around the state blasted the decision.

The *Meridian Daily Star* wrote, "Accepting the bid would constitute a breach in the walls of segregation.... We are fully aware of the loss of certain prestige by not playing integrated teams. However, as dear as the athletic prestige of our schools may be, our southern way of life in infinitely more precious."

The reaction of the *Jackson Daily News* was worse: "The decision is diluting a principle that wise men of Mississippi inaugurated years ago for valid, tested reasons. All the hysterical harping over a crack at a mythical national championship isn't worth subjecting young Mississippians to the switch-blade-knife society that integration inevitably spawns."

There's not much ambiguity there.

The reaction didn't deter the MSU leadership, but a fire-breathing state senator named Billy Mitts, ironically a former Mississippi State cheerleader and student-body president, wasn't going to give up easily. He introduced a bill that would pull state funding from any institution that violated the unwritten rule.

But Colvard, Walker and McCarthy were not to be deterred. And the time required to enact such legislation would take far too long. So Mitts asked for—and received—an injunction prohibiting the trio from flying out of the state on the day the team's flight was scheduled to leave Starkville for Lansing, Mich., the site of their first-round game against eventual national champion Loyola (Ill.) University. It was a classic battle of strong wills.

Colvard moved up a previously scheduled trip to Alabama and left the day before, by car. Walker and McCarthy drove to Nashville the night before the scheduled flight, leaving behind the team with an assistant coach and the sports information director. Since the injunction was only against Colvard, Walker and McCarthy, the sheriff allowed the team to board the plane in Starkville. It stopped in Nashville and picked up Walker and McCarthy, then went on to Lansing.

The result of the game did not go Mississippi State's way. Worn out from almost two weeks of anxiety and uncertainty, and maybe rusty from a lack of practicing when they didn't know if they would be allowed to play, the Bulldogs lost 61-51 in that opening game. They beat Bowling Green in the consolation game the next night.

The Bulldogs coaches and players were hopeful that their adventure would not make them the subject of more protests when they returned to Starkville the next day. In fact, the opposite happened. Their flight was met by more than 1,000 cheering fans. That is ironic, because the previous fall, there were numerous riots in Oxford, Miss., when the University of Mississippi enrolled James Meredith, the first Black student at the school.

Maybe because of the courage displayed by the three men responsible for MSU's participation in the 1963 NCAA Men's Basketball Championship, when Mississippi State enrolled its first Black student a year and a half later, there were no riots. It barely made the newspapers.

This is a great example of how sports can be a conduit for change in the issue of racial unity. Unfortunately, there are plenty of examples where sports can help perpetuate racism.

There's the perception that the only legal way out of "the hood" is to excel in sports or music/entertainment. Take a look at the major professional sports leagues. Approximately three out of every four NBA players are Black. Nearly 70 percent of NFL players are Black. Major League Baseball has a large Hispanic contingent (nearly 30 percent), but fewer than 10 percent are Black. That number has dropped in the past 20 years from an all-time high of 18 percent. But there's still a huge Black influence in professional sports.

The leagues could do something about it, by promoting the fact that only a small percentage of even high-level college athletes play professionally and therefore all kids should focus on academics and other pursuits as well. But they have little or no interest in that. These are huge money machines, and they don't want to dilute the number of "applicants."

College athletics is no different from professional sports. The money is so big, the coaches have to win to keep their jobs. They usually don't care about their star player's GPA. As long as he is eligible, he's useful. This is not just a Black issue. It's true with all races. White, Hispanic, Asian, all the races can be "abused" in this way.

Before you say I'm opposed to the impact that sports has in our society, remember that I have made a living as a coach. So I believe in the value of sports for developing young men and women into vital parts of society.

But the misconception that sports are an easy way out of "the 'Hood" is still very prevalent. Parents see their kid excelling in Little League sports and they think the kid will be their meal-ticket out of poverty. The kids see the poverty around them and then see the success that the professional athletes are having. They don't see the success that Black business leaders or executives have, because they're not publicized.

It's probably true in all walks of life, but in the Black communities there are not enough good examples of people who have achieved outside of the public eye. They don't see enough examples like Ben Carson, a heart doctor who ran for President in 2016. And sometimes, when Blacks do try to achieve, they are accused by their fellow Blacks of "trying to be White." The all-too-common attitude is that the White man's way is through hard work and sacrifice, while the Black man's way is through sports, music and entertainment, or dealing drugs.

It's almost ludicrous that this attitude is still out there, but it is. It leads to an "us vs. them" attitude that further divides the races.

Some sports organizations have tried to change things to even up the opportunities for minorities. For example, the NFL has the "Rooney Rule," which requires that NFL teams interview at least one Black coaching candidate every time there's a head-coaching vacancy. But the practicality of that is that most general managers know who they want to hire before the position even opens. They go through the process, including bringing in minority candidates. But unless he's the one the GM has picked, he really has no chance.

I'm not saying this rule is bad. It's just not practical. Just like we said previously, you can't legislate morality and you can't legislate equality. We have to get past the stereotypes and preconceived ideas that Blacks can't achieve in certain walks of life. Just like we're mostly past the idea that Blacks can't play quarterback, we have to look at coaches like Mike Tomlin of the Pittsburgh Steelers, and David Shaw of Stanford as successful football coaches, rather than successful *Black* football coaches.

Until then, Black assistants will continue to struggle to get the same opportunities as their White counterparts. I had the honor of coaching recently in the Kansas vs. Missouri high school football all-star game. I was picked as the receivers coach, but I was the only coach on my team who was not given authority to coach the players under his watch. While the running backs coach got to coach the running backs, etc., I was never allowed to work with the receivers, despite asking to work with them. My Black head on the sideline looked like inclusion. It was purely symbolic after all. At another school where I was an assistant coach, I believe I had more experience than all of them put together, but was treated like a manager, not a coach.

Sports has been an integral part of Greg's life from an early age. He was part of the All-Missouri Freestyle Wrestling team in 1975.

It's impossible to say that this happened because I'm Black, but it easily could be assumed that is the case. NFL coaches like Lovie Smith and Art Shell (with a 54-38 career record) had short stints as head coaches, but was it because they're Black that they were held to a higher standard? It's hard to say, but a lot of the evidence says it's true. Every coach in the NFL has a short leash, but I believe that Black coaches have shorter leashes than White coaches do. Again, it's impossible to prove that it's because they're Black, but I believe that still plays a role.

Let me give you another personal example. A few years ago I was hired to be the wrestling coach at a magnet school in the Kansas City area. A magnet school is supposed to bring in the best of the best from around the Kansas City Missouri School District to help them with college prep. They wanted to start a wrestling program and attract suburban Whites to the inner-city. In the interview, they asked me how I would handle it if my team was made up entirely of White wrestlers. I wondered if it was a trick question. I said, "I don't care if the team is all Chinese, we're going to dominate." I don't know if that was the right answer, but that was the way I felt. I can and have worked with anyone. Anyway, I got the job. We had all kinds of kids on the team, and we did well. We had one state champion and five all-state wrestlers within a short period of time.

I also got to coach baseball at this school. Baseball was so bad, no one wanted to coach it. After four years, we were the No. 2 team in the district. How did we get so much better? First of all, we had very good raw talent with very smart kids. We also were blessed with some amazing volunteers. Kenny Walton, who played baseball at Kansas, volunteered to love on those kids and provide leadership. Royals legend Frank White provided equipment and helped coach technique to our infielders. As in any successful program, we had great parental support. Finally, I know how to stretch kids to help them excel. I've always enjoyed putting an "I Can" attitude in the spirit of athletes.

At that time, the school was looking for a football coach. Just like baseball, the football program was horrible. I told them I would coach football as well, so I served as interim head coach during the summer. I worked with the kids in 7-on-7 drills, with weight training and with overall conditioning. We were going to have a very good team. I had some excellent coaches who had agreed to assist me. These men were great at coaching, and motivating kids to shine.

Right before the season started they hired someone else. He was a very negative guy, who destroyed the spirit of the kids, and the program suffered. He didn't last long, but instead of hiring me, they hired a different coach. He was a young Black guy who seemed to be very angry and militant.

I served as his offensive coordinator and we started to improve again. One day, he called me into his office on a Saturday early in the season. He wrote "Black" on the chalkboard and drew a line straight down the middle. I was very confused and didn't understand where he was going with it.

'RISE ABOVE ADVERSITY'

We had an opportunity to sit down with Bob Kendrick, the president of the Negro Leagues Baseball Museum, and discuss our premise for this book. Bob agreed with us on the basic idea that this is not a Black vs. White issue, or a Hispanic issue or an Asian issue. It's not an economic issue, or a demographic issue. It's a sin issue, an issue of the heart.

The Negro Leagues Baseball Museum exists to commemorate one of the darkest periods in American sports, the segregation of our National Pastime. Kendrick and his staff do an outstanding job of commemorating it in a way that speaks to the solutions we've discussed in these chapters.

He told me, "That's you. You should only be helping the Black kids." I wanted to help the Blacks, the Whites, the Hispanics, the Asians and any other group that wanted to work for championships. I wanted to help everybody. But it offended him that I was helping everybody. He said, "After hundreds of years of prejudice in our country, it's time to make things even. You need to focus on helping the Black kids only." I disagreed, and told him that I felt like we should give our best effort to help every kid. He didn't agree, and I was no longer allowed to coach football there.

It's not a one-way street. Blacks have bigotry in their hearts too. Whether it's thinking that they're better than Whites, or feeling animosity toward Whites for the way their ancestors were treated, they're out to "make things right" by doing the wrong thing.

Another example of racism that's way too prevalent in sports is the idea of tokenism. Just like the Rooney Rule, where the NFL is trying to even up things, it's being done in a racially biased way. The plan is a

Here is a look at our conversation.

> *GT:* **What do you say when you see young kids, especially White kids, wearing NLBM gear? They have no clue about how bad things were and why the Negro Leagues even existed.**

> *BK:* There should not have been a need for the Negro Leagues, but the way we treat this story here is unique. Sometimes people come here and expect to be introduced to a sad, somber story. They know that this story is related to ugliness of American segregation, a horrible chapter in American history.

good idea; figure out a way to have the industry—in this case sports—reflect the general population to a degree.

Our country was not founded on equality, even though our Declaration of Independence says "all men are created equal." Inequality is not fair or right. That's why programs like Affirmative Action were created. If two candidates are equally qualified, I think it would be fair to pick the Black candidate to even things up a little. But to pick somebody strictly because he or she is Black is no more right in principle than to *not pick* someone because he or she is Black.

About 15 years ago, a prominent White suburban coach came to me and said, "I need a Black coach." When he told me that I wondered what position he needed to fill. Did he need a running backs coach or a linebackers coach? He didn't need a particular position, he just needed a Black head on the sidelines. He wanted to give the appearance of diversity.

> The way that we frame the story is not about segregation, not about the adversity, but about what these men were able to do to rise above that adversity. That's the real story. This is not a 'woe is me' story. It's a triumphant story. It is, in essence, the power of the human spirit to persevere: You won't let me play with you? Then I'll just create a league of my own.
>
> If you stop to think about that, it's the American spirit at its absolute best. Even though it was America that was trying to prevent men from sharing in the joys of her so-called National Pastime, it was the American spirit that allowed them to persevere and prevail. They rose above the acids of

The double-standard translates to players too. You're accepted for the most part if you can dunk a basketball or catch a football. But I don't believe the same type of help is offered to the average Black athletes at many of our major colleges as is available to the average White athlete. Similarly, Black athletes who help win national championships, like Cam Newton at Auburn or Vince Young at Texas, are treated like kings. On the outside, people might say, "they're all treated the same." But if you're a marginal player, it's generally not the same.

It also applies to what positions athletes play. In all levels of football, you're either a quarterback or a Black quarterback. The prevailing thought has been that if the quarterback is Black, he's like Michael Vick; if he's White, he's like Peyton Manning, or Tom Brady, or Drew Brees, or Phillip Rivers, all of whom have a variety of skills. Black quarterbacks? They're perceived as running quarterbacks.

Early in the 2016 college football season, there was a great match-up of undefeated teams. No. 3 Louisville played at No. 6 Clemson. Both

American segregation. They weren't going to be denied the opportunity to play the game they loved.

What better way to show them than to create their own league that rivaled, and in some cities, surpassed Major League Baseball in popularity and attendance. They weren't as well financed, but the play on the field was as good as any.

What bothers me the most is when people say 'It's too bad that nobody saw them play.' There were a lot of people who saw them play. It was mainstream America that missed out on some of the best baseball ever played in this country. You can see that by seeing the impact of those who transitioned to the schools have Black quarterbacks, but their styles couldn't be more different. Louisville quarterback Lamar Jackson is the prototypical dual-threat quarterback, just as much a threat to run as he is to throw, but he has a great arm. Clemson quarterback Deshaun Watson is more of a pro-style quarterback, who will always look to pass first. He can run, and will when the opportunity is there, much like Alex Smith, the White quarterback of the Kansas City Chiefs.

The media, for the most part, was all over the fact that two Black quarterbacks were squaring off against each other in a game in the deep South, and spent their time talking about how they were alike, rather than how they were different. They're both athletes—not Black athletes—just athletes.

It's not just the fans or the media who have this gross generalization. I think it's evident at all levels of coaching. If you're a coach at a suburban high school and a 6-3 Black kid shows up at your school, you're likely thinking "He's a basketball player." With a White kid exactly the same size, you're likely thinking, "He's our next starting quarterback."

Major Leagues. There were plenty of games between the Negro Leagues stars and the stars from Major Leagues, and they're well-documented. The record books bear out that the Black all-star teams won about 75 percent of those games. There was never any doubt about their ability to play in the Major Leagues. It was simply the social conditions of our time—and fear—that kept them out of the game.

When people come here, many don't know that Jackie Robinson played in the Negro Leagues. They learn that Jackie, Ernie Banks, Hank Aaron, Willie Mays, Monte Irvin, all of these guys who became great stars came out of the Negro Leagues. That's just a sample of the talent that was in the Negro Leagues.

Both Nate (#2) and Jon (#27) played football at Pittsburg State University, which has made Greg a Gorilla for life.

Speaking of quarterbacks, there's one quarterback who has gotten a lot more publicity in 2016 for what he said and did off the field than he did on the field, and that's Colin Kaepernick. He decided in the preseason that he would not stand during the National Anthem as a protest to the way Black people are being treated by predominantly White police forces around the country.

When you look at those pictures from the 1940s, you'll see Black and White fans sitting side by side watching the best baseball being played in this country. A lot of people believe that the Major Leagues were better, because that's what you heard about.

People now are just starting to learn about the history of the Negro Leagues. But there's nothing sad about the Negro Leagues, outside of the fact that they never should have been. All the great stars should have been able to take the field together. How much better would our game have been if there was no segregation.

GT: **Buck O'Neil used his platform in sports, as a Negro**

Many of the athletes who have supported him by joining in the protest at their own games are Black, and that perpetuates the Black vs. White antagonism. If Eli Manning were to do the same thing, the reaction would be totally different.

I think there may have been better ways for Kaepernick to protest, because the backlash against him labeled him as anti-military. That was not the case. But think back about Dr. Martin Luther King, Jr. Mainstream society told him that his protest was all wrong. But he did what he needed to do to make his point.

With Kaepernick, I'm concerned about how easily it is to get off-topic. People have perceived him as anti-military or anti-American, which is not the case at all. And, other causes—like the gay and lesbian community—have hijacked the protest to put the spotlight on their agendas. There are too many ways to pervert the message.

The other thing is that it's impossible to determine when to stop this

Leagues player, and a coach and scout in the Major Leagues after that, to be a conduit to healing. What are your recollections of Buck using that platform?

BK: Relative to the baseball playing aspect of things, one of the most difficult things for people who come to visit us here at the Negro Leagues Baseball Museum to understand is that there were two professional baseball leagues operating at the same time. The one, Major League Baseball, everybody knew about, and we have a place to turn to learn about it. It gave the best White players the opportunities to showcase their world-class ball-playing skills.

particular protest. What statistic can you point to to say that Blacks are being treated fairly? People—Black and White—don't want to be held accountable for their actions. They will keep breaking laws and the police will need to enforce those laws. If you're Kaepernick, when do you say it's time to stop protesting because all the victims are now deserving of the treatment they're receiving?

It's all about perception. Former North Carolina State basketball coach Jim Valvano said, "Perception is more important than reality." It's time to change the false perception. It's time to start looking at solutions.

Fortunately, there are plenty of examples of how sports can be a conduit to breaking the stranglehold of racism. Besides the story of Mississippi State at the beginning of this chapter, there is the case of Texas Western (now University of Texas, El Paso) in 1966. The Miners were the first college basketball champion to start five Black players. There were other schools decades earlier that had Black players, but this was the first time all five starters were Black.

The other, the Negro Leagues, did the exact same thing for Black and Hispanic players. Both leagues were professional and they were running simultaneously. For the majority of baseball fans, if it didn't happen in the Major Leagues it didn't happen. I don't think any of the players in the Negro Leagues, including Buck, subscribed to that belief. You could not convince them that they were not playing the best baseball that was being played in this country.

The world may have thought the best baseball was being played in the Major Leagues, because they didn't see these guys play. But those who did see them play, had a different perspective. Major League Baseball, again, was better financed, but

Ironically, the opponent was the most successful college basketball program of all-time to that point, the University of Kentucky. Kentucky was ahead of its time in the Southeastern Conference in its willingness to play against teams with Black players, but the game marked a significant point in the integration of college athletics.

Probably the most famous example of sports leading the way was the integration of Major League Baseball when Branch Rickey signed Jackie Robinson out of the Negro Leagues to play for the Brooklyn Dodgers. We don't have room to tell the whole story here, but let me give a brief synopsis.

A White man, Branch Rickey, was the general manager of the Dodgers. Maybe because he recognized the untapped resource of the Negro Leagues but Rickey took a big risk by bringing Robinson into Major League Baseball. That story is well-documented, but the story of Pee Wee Reese is a great example of sports leading the way.

Reese was raised in racially segregated Kentucky, no doubt exposed to

with the play on the field, the Negro Leagues wouldn't take a back seat to anybody.

Buck's opinion was always, "Don't feel sorry for me because I didn't play in the Major Leagues. Feel sorry for the people who didn't see me play. They're the ones who missed out." I think a majority of the players carried that same perspective.

Playing in the Major Leagues for those players was far-fetched. They didn't start thinking about playing in the Major Leagues until Jackie Robinson broke the color barrier. Prior to that, it was just accepted that we had these two separate strong racist opinions. Yet when Robinson became his teammate with the Dodgers, Reese was one of the first to welcome him.

Wikipedia tells the story this way: "Reese was a strong supporter and good friend of the first 20th century black Major League Baseball player, Jackie Robinson. He was serving a stint in the Navy when the news of Robinson's signing came. Although he had little or no experience interacting with minorities—according to Reese, his meeting Robinson marked the first time in his life that he had shaken hands with a black man—he had no particular prejudices, either.

"It is reported that his father had made him starkly aware of racial injustice by showing him a tree where a lynching had occurred. The modest Reese, who typically downplayed his pioneering role in helping to ease the breaking of the 60-year-old color line, said that his primary concern with regard to Robinson's arrival was the possibility of Reese losing his shortstop job. Robinson was assigned to play as the team's first baseman, and Reese retained his position.

leagues, two separate worlds. That was the byproduct of a segregated world.

What I find so amazing is, to a man, Buck included, none of these guys harbored bitterness toward anything that happened in their lives. I find that to be an amazing quality. Had they been bitter, we would have said they had a right to be bitter. None of these men were bitter, and it goes back to the fact that they thought they were playing the best baseball in the world.

They didn't harbor any ill will toward these people who did these heinous things against them. They would go into a town

"Reese refused to sign a petition that threatened a boycott if Robinson joined the team. When a sportswriter asked Reese if he was threatened by Robinson taking his position of shortstop, Reese simply responded, 'If he can take my job, he's entitled to it.' When Robinson joined the Dodgers in 1947 and traveled with them during their first road trip, he was heckled by fans in Cincinnati. During pre-game infield practice at Crosley Field (the then-home of the Cincinnati Reds, Reese, the captain of the team, went over to Robinson, engaged him in conversation, and put his arm around his shoulder in a gesture of support which silenced the crowd."

I'm sure the fact that he knew that Pee Wee Reese was in his corner helped give Jackie the courage to withstand the taunts, abuse and discrimination that he received constantly. I think that was huge, and that probably wasn't played up enough.

It not only helped Jackie deal with the situation, I believe it also helped our country take the first steps toward looking at him as a baseball

and fill up the ballpark, yet not be able to get a meal from the same fans who just cheered them, or find a place to stay. They were relegated to sleeping on the bus and eating peanut butter and crackers. Somehow, there was an underlying motivation to rise above that and say, "So be it. I'm going to keep playing ball. You can't take the joy of playing baseball away from me."

GT: **You said it earlier: we shouldn't have a NLBM because there shouldn't have had to be Negro Leagues Baseball. With that in mind, how did they not get bitter?**

BK: I don't know where that comes from. It is an amazing thing to be around them, because they'll tell you, "I made my living player, not a Black baseball player. He won the Rookie of the Year award in 1947, and the Most Valuable Player award two years later. I'm surprised he won those awards, but I believe that Reese's acceptance played a big role.

Another well-documented story is the friendship between NFL Hall of Famer Gale Sayers and his teammate with the Chicago Bears, Brian Piccolo. Both were rookie running backs in the same season, and they couldn't have had more different personalities. Sayers, a Black man from the University of Kansas, was reserved, while Piccolo, a White man from Wake Forest University in North Carolina, was outgoing and outspoken.

The two became close friends during their brief, shared careers. The key was that they got to know each other. They didn't assume the stereotypes.

The story of Sayers' support during Piccolo's battle with and subsequent death from cancer was documented in the movie "Brian's Song."

playing baseball. I got paid to do what I love to do." They didn't make as much money as their White counterparts, but they were able to see the world playing baseball.

Buck talked about that. He made his living in baseball for seven decades. He said he never had a job in his life. That spirit, that ability to forgive, to not hold on to hate, Buck referred to it as "agape." Buck would quote Dr. Martin Luther King Jr. in saying that agape is an overflowing love that does not require anything in return. Theologians will tell you that is the love of God operating in a human heart.

When you reach love on that level, you love all men, not

It's a great example of how a grass-roots effort, not something legislated from some organization, impacted a team and a community. And with the success of the movie, it impacted the entire country.

An easy example of sports bridging the gap is any NFL stadium on a Sunday afternoon in the fall. When the home team does something great, the fans go crazy. They celebrate with high-fives with total strangers, and the race of the other person does not matter. It's not the color of their skin; it's the color of their jersey. The same is true in college football, professional baseball and practically any sports setting.

The final example I want to discuss is Hank Aaron's pursuit of Babe Ruth's career home run record in late 1973 and the beginning of 1974. Aaron, a Black man raised in Mobile, Ala., and a short-time veteran of the Negro Leagues, was a victim of racist comments, hate mail and even death threats. While his counterpart, Willie Mays, was well-received in mainstream America, Aaron was not.

because you like them, not because their ways appeal to you, but because God loves them.

That was the premise for Buck, and the premise for many of those who played in the Negro Leagues. Buck would say, "I can't hate another human being, because that's God's creature. And God didn't make anything ugly. Now you can get ugly, and this world can make you ugly. But God didn't make you ugly."

Buck was a very spiritual man. I think many of these guys were, from the standpoint that you had to have faith to endure and deal with some of the things they had to deal with.

As he approached the record he was insulted by then-commissioner Bowie Kuhn, who said he would not be in attendance when Aaron broke the record. The most hallowed of all baseball statistics was being chased, and Kuhn didn't think it was worth a break from his schedule to be there.

When Aaron hit his 715th home run, breaking Ruth's record in front of a sellout crowd in Atlanta April 8, 1974, the Braves announcer Milo Hamilton said, "There's a new home run champion, and it's Henry Aaron." Interestingly, the Dodgers announcer was legendary broadcaster Vin Scully, who said. "What a marvelous moment for baseball. What a marvelous moment for Atlanta and the state of Georgia. What a marvelous moment for the country and the world. A Black man is getting a standing ovation in the Deep South for breaking the record of an all-time baseball idol."

Leave it to Vin Scully to wrap it up so beautifully.

Baseball became their sanctuary. Even when they were able to transition to the Major Leagues, it was still very difficult being in an environment where nobody wanted you to be there. All those guys had to have faith in some form or fashion. It allowed them to look past the perpetrator of these terrible acts and look at them as an individual.

GT: **How can sports be a part of healing from racism?**

BK: I think sports has been the thing that has brought us together more than any other thing in our society. Sports has been a tremendous barrier-breaker. It goes from Joe Louis to Jesse Owens to Jackie Robinson, eventually to Muhammed Ali, who

So what can we learn from these examples? It's pretty much the same thing we've been saying from the beginning of this book: look past the differences and focus on the similarities. We're all different, but we're all human beings and we all have value.

We have to look introspectively and decide if we're excluding anybody because of the color of their skin or any other factor that shouldn't have any impact at all. These decisions may not be as drastic or as obvious as the segregation of Major League Baseball. But if those decisions are happening, they are damaging to our goal of equality.

We all bring our own experiences, both positive and negative. A coach—actually any adult who has influence on a young person's life can, and should, take into consideration the struggles that the young person has been through. If that kid doesn't know where he's going to sleep that night because one parent is in jail and the other is nowhere around, it will be really hard to concentrate during practice or team meetings. The same is true in the classroom at school.

took a less than popular stance politically, but then became one of the most beloved athletes in American sports history.

This museum makes the bold assertion that Jackie Robinson's breaking of the color barrier was not just part of the Civil Rights Movement, it was the *beginning* of the Civil Rights Movement. It was before the notable Civil Rights occurrences like Brown vs. the Board of Education and Rosa Parks' refusal to move to the back of the bus.

Dr. Martin Luther King Jr., as Buck would so eloquently say, was a sophomore at Morehouse College when Robinson signed his contract to play for the Brooklyn Dodgers. President

**Chip Sherman is a great example of the impact
a coach can have on his or her players.**

Truman did not integrate the U.S. military until a year after
Jackie. For all intents and purposes, that is what started the ball
of social progress rolling in our country.

Our country literally jumped on the coattails of baseball.
Even though Major League Baseball has been vilified for not
allowing Blacks to play, when it opened its doors, our country
followed suit when that barrier was broken. The reverence that
baseball held, and still holds, in our society is immense.

Just go back one year ago. Eight hundred thousand people gathered to celebrate the Kansas City Royals winning the
World Series, 800,000 people of every race and color. It was an

Knowing these situations can help the adult leader focus specific attention to help that kid. I'm not suggesting that every coach "adopt" every troubled youth. But the key is to not make everybody fit into the same box. Just like all Black kids who want to play quarterback aren't going to be dual-threat quarterbacks, not every kid has a peaceful life at home.

It's a sticky situation. We must look at each other as equals, but at the same time know when and how to make adjustments based on circumstances. It's no different than changing to a pass play when the defense stacks the box. It would be foolish to try to run the ball against an eight-man box, and it would be foolish to try to treat every individual as if they had the exact same life experiences.

We can be proactive. Recruiting can give opportunities for kids who might not be able to afford college to get that chance. Hopefully, those opportunities are based on the ability to help the team win, not on the color of their skin.

amazing thing to witness. That's what we've seen in the history of this country as it relates to sports.

Sports is the one area in our society where the rules are clear and apparent, and they're enforced that way. Three strikes and you're out. Four balls and you get to take a base. In the private sector and in the business community, the rules aren't always the same for everybody. In sports, the rules are exactly the same for everybody, and I think that's why you've seen so much success in this area through sports.

It would it be safe to say, "Let's not try to figure out how sports can be part of the healing. Sports can be part of the

Helping kids from all parts of our country get ready for college is everybody's responsibility. There's nothing keeping Whites from working in the inner-cities or mentoring kids from the inner-cities like Coach Chuck Sears did for me when I was in high school. He coached out in the suburbs, but he took this young, Black, inexperienced wrestler and help him become very successful on the mat and in life.

There are plenty of camps and clinics that blend the kids from different races and different backgrounds, where they receive coaching from adults from different races and different backgrounds. I worked for several years for the Fellowship of Christian Athletes. Each summer, thousands of kids from all walks of life attend camps across the country. Most of these camps are sports-specific, while there are some that let the kids play a variety of sports.

All the camps focus on helping the kids develop a new or enhanced relationship with Jesus Christ. For as long as I've been involved with FCA, first as a camper in high school, then as a college huddle leader, then a coach and finally as an employee, the focus has been on viewing each of us as created in the image of God.

Sports can be the ultimate ice-breaker in situations where there is

healing, so let's jump on and go for a ride." Sports has been part of the healing. I don't know any other thing that has brought us together the way sports has.

People of all races sat around the radio to listen to Joe Louis fight Max Schmelling in 1936 and again in 1938. But away from the ring, or the track in the case of Jesse Owens, they were still Black. Sports has helped with the healing. It didn't get rid of all the wounds of our country. But it started it.

tension. Whether it's racial, political or any other type of tension, roll a ball out onto a field and kids will figure out a game to play. We can use that almost-universal passion for sports to bridge the racial gap.

It's time to drop the guilt and be a part of change. The ball is in your hands.

Chapter 6

EDUCATION

THERE ARE SERIOUS gaps between areas that are inhabited primarily by minorities versus those inhabited primarily by Whites.

One of the most obvious areas is education. It's well-known that the inner-city schools are less-funded and less-resourced than suburban schools. The teachers generally make less money, and the teachers who are there to make a difference are outnumbered by those who are simply looking for experience so they can move on to bigger and better things.

The teachers in inner-city schools have their work cut out for them. Here are a few staggering statistics. In middle class neighborhoods, there are an average of 13 book titles for every child. In lower-income neighborhoods, there is one book title for every 300 children. Before they start kindergarten, children from middle-income families read an average of 1,350 hours. Children from low-income families read an average of 25 hours.

Do you want more? Children with as few as 25 books in the household completed an average of two more years in school than children raised in homes without any books.

With those statistics in mind, it might not be fair to condemn the school districts in poorer parts of town for not teaching the kids well enough. They're starting from much further back, from the very beginning of a child's educational path.

But that doesn't mean that the gap can't be narrowed, or even eliminated. It's going to be a very tough path, but one well worth the effort.

Just like the general problems with racism in our society, the impact of racism in the educational system is deeply embedded. It is so ingrained that just throwing money at it, or instituting new programs won't change it much. We must first change the underlying plan.

I believe the problem goes back to the days of slavery in this country. Even after it was no longer against the law for a Black person to be educated, an education generally would do you no good. There was a ceiling to what you could do. You could shine shoes or do some other entry-level or "servant type" position. Even in the North, there weren't very many opportunities for a Black man to use an education to better himself.

While the laws of racism may no longer exist, the residue of racism is still alive in our educational system. If you think you can only go so far, with or without an education, where is the motivation to do well in school? Many feel like they don't need school, as boys plan to do body work on cars and girls plan to do hair.

Fortunately, unlike sports where the solutions could impact the power structure negatively thus making it harder to force change, if we do change the culture of our educational system, everyone wins.

There's an old riddle that's appropriate here. Q: How do you eat an elephant? A: One bite at a time. We're not going to change things in one bite. The challenge is determining where to start.

When I was in college at Central Missouri State University (now the University of Central Missouri) in the education track, I took a class called Family Life. The purpose was to help students understand what their students would be experiencing in their homes (in normal daily living outside the classroom).

Routinely, my teacher would refer to the inner-city family by saying "in the Black family you have …" It was always brought up in a negative light. When she talked about the suburban and rural family, it was very pristine and healthy. It bothered me, because a lot of the things she said about Black families were not true in the family I experienced growing up. I was sure that generalizing in this way was not only unfair, but inaccurate.

One day after class, I asked her why she expressed negativity so commonly when discussing the Black family. She seemed to be oblivious to the fact that she did that. I didn't confront her the first time she did it. It happened over and over. She really seemed surprised that she gave that impression, so she asked me to bring it to her attention when she did it again. She wasn't even aware of it.

This was almost 40 years ago, so I don't remember her exact reaction when I did come back to her with an example. But her approach changed. I don't remember that I had to keep going back to her. At least I made her aware of it.

I don't blame her. She probably was passing along what she had learned in class in her own education. The approach was so ingrained into the system that it wasn't going to change easily. I'm wondering if I took that same class today, are many of those same premises still being taught? It's so much easier to go along with an accepted opinion than it is to find out if it's true and seek to change the common perception.

Are the young people in the education track in our nation's colleges being told that if you teach in the suburbs your students will be ready and anxious to learn, while the students in the inner-city schools will need to be babysat more than taught? While, to a degree that may be true, is it perpetuated because change is too difficult? And if it's true, why don't we do something to change it? Don't the kids—Black, White, Hispanic, Asian, whatever—deserve our best effort?

I've had the fortune of working in inner-city, suburban and rural settings, with public, alternative, private elite, Christian, home-school and juvenile-detention settings. I've seen the best and worst of education, and everything in between.

As a rule in my experience, it seems that the urban high schools are run very differently. In schools that primarily reach White kids, the common perception is that there are limitless possibilities. They are taught to use their educational opportunity to get to college, learn a vocation or in some other way improve themselves.

With primarily minority students, the common perception seems to be "get them in, get them through, let them go." There is an unspoken attitude that these kids aren't going to be achievers so they're not worth the effort of investing time in their education. The emphasis is not there for the students to go to college and do well. It's to survive today. Therefore, there's no expectation, from the educators or the students, that education can be used to improve their lot in life.

It's hard to blame the teachers for not wanting to fight for their students. It's tough to have to deal with a daily barrage of dysfunction. It's very sad to see the level of disrespect many kids have for hard working teachers.

Imagine if you were at your job and people regularly cursed you out, threatened you, disrupted your work environment or just wreaked havoc on a regular basis. There's little accountability. Teachers have the responsibility, but not the authority, to have order in the classroom.

I've seen this firsthand too many times. It's very hard to teach when you don't have many students wanting to learn. This is another reason why specially trained teachers for kids from very damaged life experiences need to be there in smaller classroom settings. The approach is vital to get those type of students motivated to see their future as one of a successful person with a great family that contributes to a vibrant society.

Parents need to teach their kids to have respect for authority. They can teach them to go to school with an "attitude of gratitude." They get to go to school with an opportunity to learn every single day. A generation or two ago, that was not the case.

Please don't get defensive or misunderstand me in this. I've seen great classes in some hard places, but that's been the exception, not the rule. For the most part, it seems to be a "catch-22," as parents complain about the education their child receives, while they send a child who is unmotivated to learn and is either disruptive or passive.

But getting defensive will not help. It's like someone talking about your family member in a negative light. You want to defend them, even if you know what they're doing is wrong, and you may be to a point where you think it's okay the way it is.

Sadly, the inner-city schools have the least resources, the least experienced staff (partly because the pay is lower in many cases), the fewest extra-curricular programs and the highest percentage of kids needing special help. Many things are allowed in an urban setting that wouldn't be allowed in a suburban school.

I've heard superintendents talk about "No child left behind." I want to offer a strong rebuttal. So many minority kids are being left behind! Many can't read, write or follow simple directions. In some states when a high school student is tested, if he or she can't read at a fourth-grade level, the state will budget for another jail cell. There is a direct correlation between education and incarceration.

This lack of reading or respect for education can cause great difficulty when the student is older and on the streets. A police officer may give a simple instruction and they don't obey or do just the opposite of what was instructed, just like they did years earlier in the classroom. It's obvious how that can create conflict.

Many of the districts, in urban America especially, are set up for students to fail. If you walked the halls and sat in the classrooms and saw what happens daily in many of those schools, it would rock you. Imagine your child being a student there instead of a well-organized and well-run private or suburban school. Can you imagine how different an urban school would be run if the President, Congress, school administrators, judges, etc. had to send their children to some of these tough schools. Would the language, violence, disrespect, or lack of learning be allowed? I doubt it very seriously.

Very few students get to escape the dilemma of what generally happens there. A few, who may be great in basketball, football or other sports might find a kind heart or a loophole to allow them to go to be noticed by a college that offers a scholarship. But in many cases, it's a major culture shock.

If the educational system truly served all its constituents, or if the term "Black Lives Matter" extended to education, school districts would have programs for kids who can't function well in a regular class. There would be smaller class sizes with teachers trained to deal with mentally and emotionally unstable kids who are struggling with self-worth. Much of this is due to a "Father Wound"—there is no dad to influence the kid to do the right thing in society.

It starts at home, then moves to the school and then to the community. Parents can make a huge impact here by teaching their children at an early age to go to school with the mindset to learn and serve the teacher. It will be a "win-win" for both. Much of the blame is in the home. But that's a subject for a different book.

I have to wonder where the incentive is to change this overwhelming attitude. Imagine how different inner-city schools would be if judges, doctors, attorneys, company executives and politicians *had to* put their kid in those schools.

What would the expectation be for the classroom environment? What would happen if kids had to reach "benchmarks" for achievement? Do you think kids would be allowed to come in and out of class at will, with the constant threat of violence, with drugs being sold in the restroom? Would teachers be attacked and cursed out regularly while kids play video games and dominoes instead of doing classwork?

This is not a Hollywood script writer trying to paint a picture of dysfunction in the school setting. It's real, and it's prevalent.

At one school where I taught, I commented to a teacher about "early track practice," as kids raced down the halls to avoid security officers. At another school, I told the kids it was not a mall, it's a school. You can't just wander in and out at will and huddle to discuss "Judge Judy type stuff" instead of paying attention to the teacher and taking notes.

Too many kids have to go junior college instead of a four-year college to compete in athletics because they have a low GPA or score on their

ACT. They blame the teacher, the school, the school district, President Obama, or anyone they can think of, because it's easier to blame others than to take responsibility for yourself. It's also very believable when a student blames the situation, because to a huge degree the system is set up for the average inner-city kid to fail.

I worked in the adult correction system and in the juvenile detention system. I've had many discussions with casualties of this system. I've spent time asking about their schools and how they functioned within them. It wasn't intended for research for this book, but to figure a better way of helping kids at the bottom who are crying out for help in inappropriate ways.

It's not about the government giving them more money for a new weight room, football field or new uniforms. All of those are good, but those aren't the solution. It's to help kids overcome home dysfunction. If you can empathize what it'd be like to either be fully or even semi-homeless, without any good role models or anyone telling you "You can do this," you might be able to reach the kid where he or she is.

So many in our society have no idea how bad it really is. Their perception of the inner-city is what they see on television or in the movies. There was an outstanding movie that came out in 2007 called *Freedom Writers*. It starred Hillary Swank as a White, fresh-out-of-college teacher in the inner-city who was appalled at the lack of interest in education by her students.

Without giving away too much of the plot (you should watch it for yourself), Swank's character changed the lives of the students by convincing them that a better life was possible if they applied themselves.

The setting of the movie is upsetting for Middle Class America, but it doesn't begin to tell the story of how hopeless the situation is for many kids in similar settings in the inner-cities of America. Through mainstream media, we are told, "Everything is pretty good. Just pull yourself up by your bootstraps if you have it tough."

I remember growing up in the mid 1960's watching television shows like *Batman, Leave It To Beaver* and *The Beverly Hillbillies*. I hardly ever saw any Black people in those shows, other than in a subservient role. Occasionally I'd see Bill Cosby, Sidney Poitier or Sammy Davis, Jr., but it was rare.

In a way, I felt like I didn't exist. It was a weird feeling to see them. Imagine if you lived in China and only saw Chinese people on television. How would you feel? Would you feel like an outsider? Or worse? If you can empathize with this, you can begin to see how some Blacks may feel.

So what can we do? How about teaching real-life subjects. I was in one "magnet" school, where the curriculum was geared toward teaching the Black students about African history. Instead, I would suggest teaching them how to balance a checkbook, how to budget their time so they can be on time for work, or how to fill out a job or loan application. Why don't we teach them how to save and invest, why taxes are needed, and what insurance needs they might have as an adult? Many of these students have no idea how to have a structured family, with a mom and dad to give a child the best chance for success.

Some people think you have to know where you came from to know where you're going, and there's some truth to that. But these kids didn't come from Africa. They came from the inner-city in many cases, where a lack of education forced their parents and grandparents to scrape together a living.

Finally, I think the most important change would be to change the base of the system, beginning with the family. We can teach young men that they have a responsibility to become husbands first and then dads, instead of the opposite. I know this isn't popular in modern America, but I believe this strongly. We can teach them to take responsibility for their actions.

This may rile a chunk of society, but I believe that the most important thing a coach or teacher can teach is to honor Christ in all they do. It's good to teach a subject in the classroom like Algebra, English, etc. As a coach it's great to teach kids how to catch a ball, make a tackle or hit a baseball. Those things are temporal. Even for the best athletes, at some point in their lives their careers in athletics end. The ability to honor Christ allows the student to excel as an adult, as a parent, spouse and a productive member of a community.

Our society in general has gotten so far away from teaching right from wrong. We are so afraid of offending someone, we don't differentiate between good and bad. And look where that has gotten us. I'm offended that we're allowing and promoting so much evil. We're on a severe downward spiral, and I believe we're receiving some of the "payment" for what we've done. I want America to prosper and be healthy in the same way I've wanted for my family for years.

Just like I have been discriminated against as a Black man, I have been singled out for speaking about my faith, and more importantly, trying to put it into practice.

Let me give you a few examples.

At one semi-suburban school on the Missouri side, I was the head wrestling coach and an assistant football coach. The athletic director called me into his office after three years on the job and said, "The parents don't want a Christian influence so they may be going in another direction."

At another suburban school on the Kansas side, I was an assistant football and a "para." I was called into the office by the assistant principal during my second year. He said that taking kids to FCA camp was a "cause of concern" Are you kidding me? Kids go to FCA camp to learn how to become better teammates, students and citizens. We need more of that!

At another suburban school on the Kansas side, I was the head wrestling and assistant football coach, and I was a teacher. After taking four kids to FCA Camp, the head football coach called me in to say they didn't want to have anything to do with FCA or religion. The next day he removed me from the football coaching staff. I was told I wouldn't be "a good fit." I assumed it was because of the vulgarity innuendos around the program. I told him that I'd coached at more than just Christian schools so I'd be able to function well. It made no difference.

That same principal told me to get ready for wrestling and FCA during the fall. A few days after school started, he fired me as 60 kids had signed up for the FCA Huddle. He probably felt that no one would be interested, but he was blown away by the huge turnout of kids wanting to help their school in this way.

It was very hard as I'd established a solid leadership team in wrestling during the summer. Kids were fired up and ready for a great year. This was a very sad time that rocked me deeply.

God has been taken out of our schools to a great extent, and we have stood by idly and accepted it. Until we allow His truths to be taught, like integrity, honesty, love and accountability, we will keep spiraling down the same path.

I'm talking about things like creating a culture of honor and respect. Students need to hold the teacher in high regard by coming to class with gratitude and the desire to learn. I would encourage students to seek out those who are having difficulties in any area, to love on them and help them see their value to the school.

We could stop bullying—or at least reduce it drastically—as students would see it even before a teacher. The goal would be to serve each other and do the things that enhance each other. If the older students did this, when they graduate they would be missed. Then it would be time for an underclassman to take over that role.

This seems to be a Proverbs 22:6 kind of thing. That verse says, "Start children off on the way they should go, and even when they are old they will not turn from it." I don't see how anyone in their right mind could object to teaching kids right from wrong. My faith says that right and wrong are well-defined in the Bible, but even if someone disagrees with the source of knowledge, it boggles my mind how they could object to training children in "the way they should go."

Too many kids have kids of their own and don't have the ability to give them what they need. I'm suggesting that kids wait to be married, then have their kids as they're prepared for the huge expense of time, talent and treasure needed for proper development.

I know this is very controversial as such a huge amount are born to unwed mothers. This would make a huge difference in the number of kids in hospitals, prisons, cemeteries, etc. My wife Becky and I are blessed to have three wonderful kids: BreAnn (34), Nate (31) and Jon (28), and four special grandchildren. We used some of these ideas on them and they'll do the same with their children. Our kids grew up with the privilege of knowing they were loved unconditionally and that we'd be there for their games, concerts, graduations, etc.

These are not groundbreaking ideas. They're the same ideas that Adam and Eve taught their kids. Do what's right. But just like Cain and Abel, kids have the option to choose whether they want to accept the teaching. The best thing we can do as parents is to teach them right and wrong, then demonstrate what we've taught them in our own lives.

If we do that, the educational system will get better, for Black students and for White students. And the gap between the educational experiences for both will narrow.

Our next chapter will examine how religion perpetuates racism, and how, if we follow the guidelines laid out in Scripture, religion can make an impact to bridge the gaps of racism.

Chapter 7

THE CHURCH

THE FOCUS OF this chapter is on the church in general, but we'll dig far deeper into the mainstream Christian church, those of us who are called to obey the laws of God and the will of Christ. We, above all others, should look at each other as equals, created in the image of God. That certainly has not always been the case in the church in America, and it's really not the case now in many cases.

The most segregated hour in America is 11 a.m. to noon on Sundays, the most popular time for Christians to gather for worship. It's been this way for centuries in America, and though it's becoming more common for churches to have people of different races attending the same service, it's still more an anomaly than the norm.

Let's look at some reasons behind that.

From the discovery of these shores by explorers, such as Columbus and the Pilgrims, the people doing the settling were White and any other races present either were servants already or would become servants. Native Americans, for the most part, were treated as "less than human" by the settlers, and their tribes were defeated or even destroyed completely. Those who survived were put into reservations much more constricting than their original territories.

Blacks were brought to America to be a source of cheap labor. We talked earlier in this book about how early Americans took slavery from indenture to abuse and total dehumanizing in the form of chattel slavery. Whether it was strictly because of a flawed view of man or an economically driven change of view, the White majority eventually viewed Blacks as less than human, a commodity that could be traded, sold, killed or abused for profit or pleasure.

Unfortunately, the church was front and center in that thinking. White Christians attended church for a couple of hours on Sunday mornings, then treated their slaves as "three-fifths of a human" the other 166 hours of the week. And they felt no guilt about it. It was so common, that there was no movement to change, at least in the South. There really wasn't in the North, either. For a couple hundred years after the settling of America, there were slaves in the North as well. But the treatment of slaves was a little bit better in the North.

Our founding fathers, men who are highly esteemed through history, like George Washington and Thomas Jefferson, owned slaves. I've wondered often what type of Bible our founding fathers were reading that allowed them to rationalize the things they allowed to happen.

It was a status symbol to own slaves, just like today it's a status symbol to own a BMW or Mercedes. The more slaves you had, the more successful you were, and no one, other than Blacks themselves, thought there was anything wrong with it.

Think about what we wrote in the chapter on sports regarding the Mississippi State basketball team. The prevailing thought was that Blacks and Whites were different, and it would be dangerous to mix the two in society. It wasn't because of slavery at that point. It was simply the accepted opinion. Christians and non-Christians agreed. It was the norm. It was also wrong.

The amazing thing is that the Black church grew rapidly at the same time. Black men and women worshiped the same Jesus as their White "owners" did. It would have been understandable if they had chosen any religion but the one that purported to support the treatment they received, but they didn't. There are countless stories of Blacks worshiping with their own songs while being over-worked, beaten, tortured and even killed. It's mind-boggling.

Many of those same songs that were "written" during the mid-1800s are still sung in predominantly Black churches in America today. (We say "written" in quotes, because very few Blacks could read or write, so the songs were passed along by memory until much later.)

Interestingly, many White churches sing derivations of those same songs, probably without really understanding how deep the meaning goes. These songs are timeless, with a message of freedom, not just from earthly slavery but from slavery to sin. If anyone understood the concept of breaking free from the chains, it was Black America.

There is certainly some truth to the theory that our churches today are still segregated because the vast majority of people attend church in their neighborhood, and if they live in a predominantly White neighborhood, the church attendance will reflect that. Styles of worship will impact that as well. A church in rural Oklahoma, for example, will most likely have a "country" theme to it, while a church in the heart of Detroit may have a "hip hop," "R&B" or "Gospel" theme.

There's nothing wrong with that. Churches need to be able to reach those around them with the message of the Gospel, and playing Carry

Underwood or Tim McGraw in a church in East St. Louis, Ill., probably won't bring in people from the neighborhood. The same is true with featuring Lecrae or Sup the Chemist in White suburbia.

But maybe, just maybe, mixing things up a bit would help.

Contemporary Christian music is becoming more and more blended. Recording artists like Kirk Franklin and TobyMac are a blend of different genres, and it's sometimes hard to determine the root style of their songs. Even in songs written as far back as "Jesus Freak" by DC Talk, released more than 20 years ago, there are a couple of rap segments. Do you want to blow a young person's mind? Have a middle-aged White guy do the rap from that song.

But playing a song from a completely different Christian genre as people are walking into or out of a worship service could open people's minds to other styles of worship, making it less awkward when they might encounter a believer from a different demographic.

If you're in a predominantly White, Hispanic or Asian church, try playing some Donnie McClurkin, Smokey Norful, or Fred Hammond. That would be a subtle way of saying "we respect you and honor you" to your Black neighbors.

In a predominantly Black church, you could play some Casting Crowns, Chris Tomlin or MercyMe. in the same manner. Spanish worship music also could be played so people could be exposed to artists like Julio Melgar, Danilo Montero, Soulfire Revolution

It's hard to imagine the positive impact this could have. If you've always been in the "dominant" position in your circle of influence and you reach out to others who aren't used to being heard, the impact could be profound.

I'm not suggesting that you change your worship style, but just a touch of change could be powerful to some in your midst and show tremendous respect. By the way, if your regular attendees would be offended by these subtle suggestions, it's possible that they may have a heart issue that needs to be addressed.

You never know, some of the congregation might even like it. It's a very simple thing that can be done to foster healing.

If we get it right in the church and learn to love with an agape type of love for all, people will come running to our churches. Most "nones" (people who check "none" when asked religious affiliation on surveys) don't dislike God. They dislike the hypocrisy of Christians. If we get this right—*and we must*—John 13:35 will speak loudly to people, as they'll know we are Christians by our love, not our doctrine.

Let's examine a few ways that the church is guilty in the past—and still is today—of perpetuating racism.

We already discussed the early years of our country's history, and how the church condoned slavery as an accepted practice. But slavery ended, effectively, at the end of the Civil War. However, a hundred years later, in the height of the Civil Rights movement, many churches in the South still taught that Black men and women were "less than" their White counterparts.

For generations, there was a literal line in public settings, where Blacks were not allowed to cross. Even at revivals, where the love of Christ was being preached, Blacks were required to sit in their designated area, and you know it was not the best area.

There's the story we mentioned earlier where Dr. Billy Graham telling the organizers of one of his crusades to remove the rope that separated the two races. This was in the late 1950s or early 1960s. They didn't do what he asked, so he removed the rope himself. He caught some heat for that. He invited Dr. King to offer a prayer at one of his crusades. That was a no-no!

Our church history has not been good regarding racial equality. It's certainly better than it was, even when I was growing up, but there's still plenty of room to grow.

I believe the reason that progress has been so slow in this area is because we don't want to think about it. Human beings inherently try to suppress bad memories, especially when there's guilt involved. It's easier to just say, "That was then, this is now." But we can't learn from our mistakes if we don't know what they are.

Many Jews visit the concentration camps and other historical locations in Europe to remember the Holocaust. It's very important to learn about that history so it is never forgotten. In America, we seem to not really want to remember our history, warts and all. I'm guessing that a big component is guilt. It's easy to talk about what terrible people Adolf Hitler and Joseph Stalin were. But it is much harder to remember what our ancestors did.

The past shouldn't be remembered to condemn people, but to learn from it. We can't forget what happened. George Santayana was a Spanish philosopher in the late 1800s and early 1900s. He was the person who first said the now-famous quote, "Those who cannot remember the past are condemned to repeat it."

We must acknowledge that many errors in judgment led to policies that were horrific to large segments of our society. We might not have been involved in the slave trade, either as owners or slaves, but we too have done sinful things that require forgiveness. We must never head in that direction again.

An important component is how history is brought to the attention of kids in schools. I believe strongly that there needs to be a disclaimer to remind people not to be absorbed with guilt unless you are still involved in some of those practices.

Dr. Tony Evans, world-renowned founder and senior pastor of Oak Cliff Bible Fellowship in Dallas, speaks about how about 35 or 40 years ago his family wasn't received well at a White church in the south. Years later that same church apologized and allowed him to speak there. That's a great example of not holding onto the guilt, while changing the practice that caused the pain.

Fortunately, there are a lot of good examples of the church stepping up to cause change. I define church not as the building on the corner, or an organized denomination, but the people who profess to follow God's Word (the Latin term is "Ecclesia.")

Dietrich Bonhoeffer was a German theologian and pastor who came to the United States to attend seminary. He met a fellow student, who was Black, and that student introduced him to the Abyssinian Baptist Church in Harlem. It was there that Bonhoeffer changed from an intellectual theologian to an activist dedicated to fighting injustice. He later returned to Germany, where he stood in staunch opposition to Nazism, a stance that eventually cost him his life. He willingly chose to put himself in harm's way. He made an impact on many people, not only while he was living, but in the many years since his death. He didn't waver or back down to the evil that was out there.

Wikipedia describes his resistance this way: "Bonhoeffer's promising academic and ecclesiastical career was dramatically altered with Nazi ascension to power on 30 January 1933. He was a determined opponent of the regime from its first days. Two days after Hitler was installed as Chancellor, Bonhoeffer delivered a radio address in which he attacked Hitler and warned Germany against slipping into an idolatrous cult of the *Führer* (leader), who could very well turn out to be *Verführer* (mis-leader, or seducer).

"He was cut off the air in the middle of a sentence, though it is unclear whether the newly elected Nazi regime was responsible. In April 1933, Bonhoeffer raised the first voice for church resistance to Hitler's persecution of Jews, declaring that the church must not simply "bandage the victims under the wheel, but jam the spoke in the wheel itself."

Bonhoeffer was a great example of risking everything for the cause of Christ. It's very similar to what many people—Black and White—did to oppose the mistreatment of Blacks in America. They were not content with the status quo, and were willing to fight for right, regardless of the cost to themselves.

A great example was Rev. Dr. Martin Luther King Jr., who initially didn't want to be very involved in the Civil Rights movement. He wanted to just be pastor of his small, southern church. But he decided that his desires were secondary to standing up for injustice, and it was on.

Much of the Civil Rights Movement gained momentum at the Ebenezer Baptist Church under the leadership of Dr. King. Greg felt the presence of Dr. King when he visited Ebenezer a few years ago.

RACE IN AMERICA: A CALL TO HEAL

Just like the Apostle Paul, who wrote many of his epistles from jail in Rome, Dr. King wrote some of his best work from a jail in Birmingham, Ala.

Things are changing around the U.S. I'm starting to see lots of diversity in churches. But in some cases the diversity is only in the pews. What would happen if the staff of a predominantly White church hired a teaching pastor or worship pastor who is Black—or vice versa? That would be monumental, and it's starting to happen. It needs to happen more.

Have you ever gone into a business and walked around the various offices? In many cases, you'll see one Black or Hispanic face, and the business will consider itself diversified. All the faces look the same. They don't even realize that one out of 40 does not represent diversity. Many employers have a small sign that says "Equal Opportunity Employer." I've wondered what that really means when you actually look at how it is manifested.

I applaud people who take this area very seriously. They've done many things to help foster racial reconciliation. If we want the secular world to figure out what it means to view each other as equals, to love each other because we're all created in the image of God, then we must be committed to live it out completely.

Much of the credit for the Civil Rights movement went to leaders in the church. But will the leaders in our churches today have the courage to affect change? Will they be willing to—maybe metaphorically—lay down their lives for the sake of equality? I hope so. It will take a lot of effort. But it will be well worth the effort.

I'm praying and working toward an America where we can work together and have a culture of honor and respect for each other.

We need to sing from the same hymnal, on the same page. But we don't have to sing the same part. We all have our gifts, and every one of us is unique. Let's create the most beautiful harmony this side of Heaven.

When we do that, we're on our way to healing.

Chapter 8
NEXT STEPS

WE'VE SAID FROM the beginning of this book that this is not a Black and White issue, metaphorically or literally. From the "expression" standpoint, there's not an easy answer that will work in every situation.

The recent national election results won't solve it. The Republicans won't create racial harmony, and neither will the Democrats. Remember, you can't legislate morality or equality. It's up to each one of us to make changes in our lives based on our own situations.

It's not a Black and White issue from a literal standpoint either. It's not an issue caused by Blacks being different from Whites, or Hispanics, or Asians, or Native Americans, etc. It's a sin issue. If one person looks at another person as "less than" the other person, strictly because of the color of their skin, that's just plain wrong. That is a black and white answer.

But how do we move on from here? It's time to stop philosophizing and start doing. It's a long-term problem that requires long-term solutions. Most importantly, it's more about attitude than actions. Good attitude will dictate good actions. Then we're on our way.

The first step is to take responsibility—on both sides. Whites and Blacks have to take responsibility for actions that perpetuate racism, and change those actions.

Drop the guilt, it's not your fault unless you're still acting in a racist manner. The guilt of what happened in the 1800s is not your fault. In the case of most people, the guilt for what happened in the mid 1900s is not your fault. Unless you're still doing something that perpetuates the disparity in how people are treated based on race, it's not your fault. Unfortunately, most people have a tendency to hold onto guilt for something they didn't do.

It's a really tough call. Even though we're not responsible for the wrong that was done in prior generations, we have a responsibility for doing something about it now. We can't just punt it off to the next generation. Many people, especially Whites, are benefiting from some of the things that happened in the past. I believe, in those situations, you have a responsibility to affect change.

With the inequities that exist in our schools and in the work force, we need to at least be cognizant about those things and possibly change them when given the opportunity. Awareness is key. We can't turn a blind eye to inequality and say, "I didn't do it."

You're not guilty of creating these inadequacies, but you do have a responsibility for fixing what's broken, at least in your own circle of influence.

Guilt can be an anchor that keeps you from moving toward change. It can cause you to shift blame, because it hurts too much to accept the blame yourself. "Cognitive dissonance" is a term where you block out the negative feelings to avoid feeling the blame. Instead of recognizing that bad things happen, and that those things are the reason we are where we are today, we pass the blame to someone or something else.

But that won't help the situation. Releasing the guilt frees you to say, "That wasn't my fault, but I can be part of change." Once we do that, we all have steps we can take as part of the responsibility.

Let's start with Blacks, since I am a Black man.

Blacks have to knock the chip off their shoulders. Black students can't go to school with walls up and an angry attitude. Instead, enter with the expectation of learning and gaining something that you can use, immediately or later on in life.

It's more than just students. Too many Blacks go into work with an attitude that the world is out to get them. We can't go in with a "woe is me" or "it's that guy's fault because he's White and I'm Black" attitude. We must treat each situation uniquely. Don't pass blame where it doesn't belong. Not everybody is out to get you. When you get rid of that attitude, you'll have a much better experience and be a blessing to those around you.

Greg has had the fortune of coaching a lot of young wrestlers through the years, including current police officer Jordan Nelson.

During the riots in Baltimore following the arrest and subsequent death of Freddie Gray in 2015, some of the Black protesters called for an education. I'm not sure they do in many cases. So many students go into the classroom with the attitude of getting by and doing as little as possible. Parents need to be aware of what's going on in the classroom. So many parents aren't even aware that their kids are getting straight F's, due to lack of effort. There was no way my wife and I would not know if one of our kids was struggling.

This is not a debate on whether there should have been protests in that situation in Baltimore. But the people chanting about wanting an education need to recognize that education is a two-way street. Should Blacks have the opportunity to have the same quality of education as Whites? Absolutely. Do they have a responsibility to take advantage of educational opportunities when they're there? Absolutely. Don't expect a hand-out. Be ready to work when opportunities arise.

I know this is controversial. The situation that way too many Blacks face in trying to better themselves is not fair. But no one should be able to tell you that you can't achieve something that is reachable with hard work. A lot of kids are allowed, or even taught, to just do the minimum.

Too many Blacks have the attitude that hard work is a "White" characteristic. I've seen it at so many different levels, in the classroom, in sports, even in ministry, that we have been conditioned to believe that "White is Right" and "Black is Bad." For example, if you're on the football team and you work hard and try to follow the instructions of the coach, that's not considered being Black in many circles.

If you're in the classroom and the teacher tells the class to read chapter 5. If you read chapter 5 and do the assignment, your peers might look at you and ask, or at least imply, "Are you trying to be White?" That's terrible.

My brother played college football. At times, he would sit with other guys who played the same position, rather than sitting with just Black teammates. Some of those Black teammates walked near enough for him to hear and said, "I'm a nigga." Even if you want to do the right thing, your peers still might try to drag you back into the stereotypical behavior. People are too concerned about their image or perception. If your teacher or coach gives you something that's going to help you, then you do that. You shouldn't worry about it being a White thing or a Black thing.

If you're not mad at me already, get ready. We're about to go from "preachin' to meddlin'."

A lot of the negative attitude among Blacks has to do with a father-wound. Too many Black children are born out of wedlock. I know that this happens with Whites and other races, but it's much more prevalent in the Black community, in lower socioeconomic situations.

FCA has played a key role in the lives of Greg, his sons, and many young people Greg has impacted in the Kansas City area over the past 40-plus years.

When kids grow up with a mom and a dad, they have a much better chance to living a life with advantage. Our three kids grew up with privilege as they had two loving parents who were there every day for them and made sure they had what they needed for success. We also made sure that at an early age they were taught to respect teachers and go to school ready to learn and be positive contributors.

They are all very successful today, and I imagine they greatly appreciated their teachers and administrators. This carried over into adulthood. When a kid does not have a mom and a dad, it's much harder on the parent, and it's much harder on the kid. There are others who can stand in the gap, but it's not the same as having both parents in the home.

Parents can teach their kids to have respect for authority. They can teach them to go to school with an "attitude of gratitude." They get to go to school with an opportunity to learn every single day. A generation or two ago, that was not the case.

Whites need to take responsibility as well. You might not ever have discriminated against anyone because of the color of their skin, but you most likely have benefited from racist decisions in the past. Those aren't your fault, but you can still help be a conduit for change.

I've heard the question: If you're on top, why would you want to give away your advantage? When I wrestled in college, I went from sixth on the depth chart at my weight class when I started my freshman year to the top spot. I wrestled varsity my freshman year, because I earned that spot. But what if I had just been handed that spot? Would it have been disingenuous or arrogant of me to expect to keep that spot without being challenged?

It goes against our nature to want to give away an advantage, earned or not. If you're Alabama football, why would you want to give away coaches or athletes to Alabama State in order to level the playing field? We must understand that thinking before we can figure out how to change it.

Whites are higher on the socioeconomic ladder largely because of decisions made many generations ago. It was not an advantage that was earned. In many cases, it was taken by force, for unfair reasons.

So how—or why—do we change? The main reason for Whites to desire to attempt to level the playing field, is due to a Christian worldview. In previous chapters we talked about being created in the image of God. But our country is no longer based on a Christian approach to things.

I heard a definition of sacrifice that fits here. Sacrifice is giving up something of value to you for the sake of something of greater value. If you value your fellow human being as your equal, you will find it easier to give up something of value for the sake of those needing help.

It's not really about giving things away. If your suburban school has $5,000, it's not about giving $2,000 to an inner-city school. It's about opportunity. It's about opening doors that will result in equality. Giving away things to even up the numbers won't change the attitude. Just like you can't legislate equality, you can't force it. You must first change the attitude to let it happen.

None of these solutions is going to be easy. But for the greater good of mankind, we have to consider making changes. We have to remember that things have never been equal. When slavery was abolished in the 1860s Blacks did not land on equal footing with Whites. When the North won the Civil War, Blacks no longer could be kept in slavery. But very few Blacks had an education or skills beyond manual labor. They couldn't be oppressed or abused (legally), but there were no opportunities for them to move forward. Things are certainly better than they were 150 years ago, or even 50 years ago. For that Blacks need to be grateful. But they're not where they should be. We can change that.

Speaking of gratitude, I believe we all should have some gratitude for what we have. There's an expression that's true for all races, all Americans. It goes like this: "How much is enough? A little more than I have."

Greg is blessed to have some special women in his life, including Becky, Bre and her daughters Bailey and Ellie.

That is not a Christian attitude. The Lord's Prayer does not say, "Give us this day all we ask for," or "Give us this day more than my coworker has," or "Give us this day more than I had yesterday." It says, "Give us this day our daily bread." In other words, we're asking God to give us only what we need. It's okay to strive for things we don't have, but we must be grateful for what we do have.

It's not a Black or White thought. Each one of us has struggles, regardless of the color of our skin. But if we can be grateful for what we do have, it will be easier to look at equality through a better lens. If we truly look at each other as equals, we can't justify differing treatment, differing resources. There's enough to go around.

It's not about you. It's about us, a very large, collective us. It's time to put on the big-boy pants. Don't worry about image, just do the right thing. You can affect change. It will be a very tough fight, but it is, and will be, worth the effort. We can do this, if we each do our part.

It's time to heal. Do you hear the call?

CPSIA information can be obtained
at www.ICGtesting.com
Printed in the USA
FFOW05n0751281017

9 781478 782612